STILL
FOLLOWING
RAINBOWS

From the Midlands to Mull

Ray Canham

Ray Canham

Still Following Rainbows
From the Midlands to Mull

Praise for Downwardly Mobile

'A great read! The sense of humour of the author is evident throughout...If you've ever wondered why you live like you do and feel like you have the potential to swap the rat race for a more relaxing way of life you may well find this book inspiring.'

'I found myself laughing aloud on the train, to the astonishment of fellow passengers. Ray's honesty, humour and compassion - to say nothing of self-deprecating observations- contribute to a thoroughly enjoyable book.'

'I found it a real pleasure and joy to read ... and it isn't just any old travel adventure book, either. There's history, there's humour, there's behind the scenes at music festivals and you also get the laugh-out-loud family reminiscences as a side dish!'

'Great book beautifully written, made me both laugh and cry.'

'Having read a few of Ray Canham's blogs, and found them incisive, entertaining and completely honest, I was keen to read the book! It didn't disappoint. The book is interesting, sad, poignant, insightful and, in places, side-splittingly funny!'

'You could imagine yourself looking out of the window and seeing it with your own eyes, such was the way it was described. Be prepared to laugh out loud, I got some funny looks when reading this on the bus when I would chuckle and then cry in equal measure. Be sure to read this book.'

'An extremely well written book which has many laugh out loud moments and a must for anyone who loves motor homes, people watching or the wonderfully historical country we call Great Britain.'

'Canham makes the patently ridiculous idea of selling up and hitting the road seem like the most sensible life choice imaginable! ...He deftly weaves memoir, history lesson, 'how-to' festival guide and a touching love story into a book that made me alternately laugh out loud and surreptitiously wipe away a tear and generally see places I thought I knew in a completely different light.'

'After reading Downwardly Mobile I felt as if I had been along for the adventure as well. Ray's often humorous and wry perception of various aspects of human interactions coupled with the way they dealt with the range of events they attended and took part in with steadfast determination kept me enthralled.'

'I so enjoyed Ray's narrative style, and sharp wit! I would have no hesitation recommending this to anyone who wants a good laugh, insight into a care-free wayfaring life, or a lovely "traveller's guide" to some of the loveliest and quaint places in the UK, or all of the above.'

'This book takes you on a journey - not just around the country, but also inside the author's mind. It had me laughing out loud one minute and reaching for the tissues the next.'

'From a fellow van-dweller, I thoroughly enjoyed reading this book and empathised a lot! A humorous and at times poignant read, written with honesty and courage.'

'Thank you so much for a wonderful few days on the road in the shape of your book!'

'If you want to read just one funny, uplifting, touching, delightful, riotous, poignant, thoughtful, joyous book this year, make sure it's this one by the brilliantly articulate Ray Canham. Let him take you on your own journey through his.'

'We have, at times laughed uncontrollably, at others quietly reflected how beautifully, privately and sensitively your struggles have been recorded.'

'The welcomes and wonders of Britain through the eyes of two acute observers, well leavened with their healthy dose of humour.'

'Reading Downwardly Mobile made me laugh and cry, made me think and then made me want to sell our house and buy a motorhome.'

Dedication

Still Following Rainbows is dedicated to Charles and Pauline Burling and to the memory of Iris Olive Rose Canham.

Contents

Still Following Rainbows...1

Foreword 8

Introduction 10

Prologue 12

One...15

Two 20

Three...26

Four..34

Five 39

Six 43

Seven..52

Eight 58

Nine 66

Ten 75

Eleven 80

Twelve 86

Thirteen...92

Fourteen 98

Fifteen...107

Sixteen..111

Seventeen 118

Eighteen 125

Nineteen...134

Twenty 139

Twenty-One 145

Twenty-Two..156

Twenty-Three 162

Twenty-Four...166

Twenty-Five 177

Twenty-Six..184

Twenty-Seven 193

Twenty-Eight 202

Twenty-Nine 209

Epilogue 213

The Dancer..215

Acknowledgments..221

Notes..224

FOREWORD

By Adrian Nation

Singer, songwriter, activist and all-round good egg.

L
ife, is a journey. In fact, it's a ride and just as the late great Bill Hicks so eloquently reminded us, we can change it any time we like, with a simple choice.

It is easy to forget though, amid the noise and rush of modern life, that choices even exist, that there is a chance to do things differently and step beyond the bounds of convention and expectation to see what else is out there.

However, when the occasion of that choice presents itself, it takes a special kind of person to have, firstly the clarity to see it and secondly, the courage to make it.

Ray and Alison Canham are exactly those special kind of people, as Ray's first book, Downwardly Mobile so beautifully demonstrated with charm, wit and honesty.

But going back to Bill Hicks, as I can't help but do whenever I read Ray's work, he describes how life is "just a ride". How it is brightly coloured and full of spills and thrills but also how easy it is to get caught up in the worry and seriousness of it all... but, it's just a ride.

Therein lies the beauty of Ray and Alison's story. Their choices have taken them to a new life on the Isle of Mull and in every aspect of this book you will find the bright colours of life's adventure. The laughter of the every day through Ray's eyes, the anger of injustice and the deepest emotion of family are dealt with, discussed and dissolved so beautifully and humanly that it makes this a ride you just want to share.

There is a connection to be found amongst humans. You can find it in music, in art and in literature and it somehow joins you in spirit with people you may rarely and more often than not, never meet.

I was fortunate enough however, to meet Ray and Alison some years ago now whilst on my journey. The connection was made and continues, mostly from afar, but that is the joy of this life that Still Following Rainbows describes.

That chance to connect is right here in this book and turning each page is like taking another bend in the road and Ray and Alison are driving. It's their ride but they have slowed down, pulled over, (not in a designated passing place of course) and are offering you a lift.

So, the simple choice is yours.

Why not jump in?

It's just a ride....

Adrian Nation
Yukon Territory June 2019

INTRODUCTION

In 2016 my wife Alison and I tested our six-month-old marriage by resigning from good jobs, selling our house and spending eight months living in a motorhome that we christened Mavis.

On our journey we worked at music festivals where we ended up playing kazoos with a biker gang, appeared onstage with 80's pop legend Paul Young and took on the challenge of working at a large Christian festival, with unexpected results.

It became both a physical and a spiritual journey, one we undertook with precious little planning and no safety net. There was soul searching, looking back, reconnecting with estranged family, confronting of demons and searching for a place to call home.

Our adventures formed the backbone of my first book, Downwardly Mobile.

* * *

I'm not sure that we ever found somewhere we really felt was home, until we washed up on the shores of the Isle of Mull off the west coast of Scotland. We had jobs, a motorhome and...well that was pretty much it really.

We had committed to four months' work over the summer to buy a little time to consider what to do next. But our growing fondness for the island and its people led us to extend our first season and then to return for a second.

Still Following Rainbows picks up where Downwardly Mobile left off, but it can still be read as a stand-alone account about our experiences on Mull and beyond.

PROLOGUE

When I was about 14 I was trusted with a rare position of responsibility at school. Together with my friend Julian we carefully fostered the false impression that literature held an interest for us, in order to gain accreditation as library monitors. In truth Julian had discovered some saucy text in a book and was eager to find more and I wanted clandestine access to the school Xerox machine to print a punk fanzine I was involved in putting together.

After a serious talk from Mr Kennedy about the importance of our role and the mighty responsibility upon our tender young shoulders we were left to our own devices. Pretty soon my hands were stained blue-black from my surreptitious printing and Julian's were rubbed raw. It dawned on us that we should probably do a little light librarianing from time to time if we wanted to retain our positions. As Julian had just discovered the D H Lawrence section, he was eager to continue, and I was getting a growing reputation for my nifty way with the cumbersome Xerox machine.

The problem with our escapade was that neither of us had paid any attention to Mr Kennedy's induction. We had a vague idea that cataloguing was involved but until now we'd contented ourselves with just sticking the returned books back where there was a space.

The delights of Dewey or Universal Decimal Classification were unknown to us.

One day while sorting some returns onto a shelf we chanced upon our own system, one that was aesthetically pleasing, simple and unique. This would put Leiston High School on the map. In our minds eyes we saw the headlines in the local paper hailing two local schoolboy heroes. On my way home that evening I was rehearsing my first radio interview and wondering what to wear when the TV crews came calling.

The following day we set about our plan, spending as much time as possible avoiding lessons and keeping other students out while we rearranged the books to our satisfaction. Sometime around mid-afternoon we stood back, arms folded and admired our handy work. Julian disappeared to the lavatory with a copy of Cider with Rosie while I made some small adjustments and tweaked the odd spine into its proper place.

With the passage of time I'm unsure if we summoned Mr Kennedy or if he just appeared but I do distinctly remember being rather hurt at his reaction to the school library being rearranged by colour and height. We thought it provided a much more appealing sight as you entered and cheered the gloomy place up no end. Indeed, I'd go so far as to say it was a vast improvement upon the mismatched chaos he'd left behind that morning.

He wasn't angry exactly. It was more an uneasy calm that lay somewhere on the icy plains beyond fury. He stood gaping and tried to start a sentence... 'but...' (silence) ... 'I mean why would...' (slow shaking of head) ... 'how would you find...' (silence) ... 'why...why...' (claps hand to forehead) ... 'I thought you understood...' (flapping of arms) ... 'I don't know what...' (silence) ... 'Why would you do...'

Turning first to Julian and then to me he whispered:

'What were you thinking...why would someone do this?'

I learnt a valuable lesson that day about rhetorical questions.

With hindsight I probably shouldn't have launched into such an enthusiastic explanation of our system, one that gradually withered under his gaze until I stood silently looking at my grubby shoes.

Our punishment was to put everything back, which given that we had to use an antiquated system that involved reading faded numbers on the spines and occasionally looking through microfilm records to cross reference, took a lot longer than we had spent on our reorganisation. We felt it was unwise to point this out to Mr Kennedy on one of his frequent visits to check on our progress, even though to this day I maintain that ours was the superior system.

* * *

All of which may explain my absolute joy on discovering a lonely charity shop on Mull that contained an entire bookcase of second-hand books arranged by colour. I bounded up to it overcome with delight. 'Behold!' I exclaimed turning to face Alison with a sweeping gesture towards the magnificent display. Considering that Alison had just spent an entire winter re-cataloguing a theological library she controlled her enthusiasm with commendable fortitude and walked away shaking her head.

I did note that their neatly coloured bookshelves were a bit untidy, but I could just imagine their delight at me popping in every day to tutor them on the correct application of the system!

Walking out with a stack of books (four red, two black and one yellow), I remarked to Alison that this was the sort of place I could see us settling, at least for a while. Looking over the sea and to the mountains beyond she turned back to me and said. 'This could be the beginning of a new adventure.'

And it was...

ONE

First and Last

You know that you've reached a certain point in life when a Bishop introduces you to his colleagues as a vampire. I'm not sure what point in life that is exactly but it was a seminal moment in many ways, one that seemed to sum up our winter. For the purposes of clarity, and for the avoidance of angry mobs armed with pitch forks and flaming torches we have never feasted on the blood of the living, combusted at the sight of a cross and we frequently cook with garlic with no ill effects other than needing a heavier than usual dose of mouthwash in the morning. When he jokingly (we assume) introduced Alison and me as members of the undead community he was referring to us emerging from our underground lair beneath a Christian conference centre in rural Staffordshire. We were employed there over the winter as relief duty managers with a brief that largely consisted of doing whatever job needed doing.

It was a peculiar time. We had a basement flat, nicely appointed with lots of homely touches, although it lacked natural light. The only window was in a fire door at the foot of a murky flight of stairs. We had our cats for company and put a cat flap in the external door with varying results. Cat number one, who we will call Leo since that is his name, wasn't exactly at the front of the queue when brains were being handed out. I doubt he was in the correct queue in the first place. He did however conquer the cat flap with aplomb, a mastery that surprised everyone, not least himself when he magically found himself on the other side of a slamming flap with a startled look on his face. Cat number two, who doesn't deserve to be namechecked, steadfastly resisted all efforts to coerce her through it unless the flap was held open for her.

She is given to that strutting arrogance that cats do so well. In ancient Egypt she'd have been worshipped as a god and have expected no less, whereas they'd have taken one look at Leo and decided that perhaps it was time to reconsider elevating every single feline to the status of deity. That aside they provided company and an air of domesticity to our subterranean lair.

Above ground our duties were divided between us, with Alison taking a lead on administrative and librarian tasks while in a misguided attempt at gender stereotyping our boss assumed I'd know which end of a hammer one uses to rewire a plug, so my work was slanted towards caretaking and a close relationship with the first aid kit. Other responsibilities were the ones that peep out from under the 'and any other duties...' line at the foot of most job descriptions. As duty managers we covered bar work, housekeeping, reception and all manner of incidental jobs.

This suited us perfectly. After a season on the road working at festivals, and in previous careers in the sort of jobs that required taking responsibility for doing what needed to be done and if necessary, getting permission or forgiveness later, we felt at home.

One other job that came my way was cooking breakfast and lunch on Saturdays for paying guests. By cooking I mean preparing toast for breakfast and ensuring the cereals were stocked up and beverages in plentiful supply. For lunch I had to deploy everything that my years of culinary expertise could muster and prepare baked potatoes with coleslaw, grated cheese and salad. Except for once forgetting to switch the oven on, my tenure in the kitchen seemed to pass without drama. Aside from a few trifling burns the only damage I sustained was a bruised toe when the first aid kit fell on it.

Outside we got to work with volunteers who looked after the extensive grounds. One of these was Brian, (not his real name) a regular volunteer who enjoyed anything with more horsepower than safety warnings. He's been known to tip a tractor onto its side on perfectly level ground. This is quite a feat in a vehicle specifically designed to cope with the wettest, muddiest and hilliest of farm conditions. He also enjoyed a lively relationship with the chainsaw; or rather he did. Last time I was there his chainsaw privileges had been withdrawn because insurance companies take a dim view of volunteers coming in for tea and cake with less limbs than they left the house with that morning.

* * *

We had met the staff and volunteers on previous visits to the centre, but when we started working there formally, we had an uncomfortable first few days with some members of the team. Possibly they thought that we were there to spy on them because we were already friends with the managers.

The tensions were often palpable, and mistrust hung in the air. There were hurriedly shushed conversations when one of us entered a room or a snide remark in our direction; more than once we considered our options for moving on. Not because we couldn't cope with the icy politeness we were often met with, but because we had deliberately given up the world of office politics and unnecessary stress. In the gloom of damp evenings in our flat we found that we were taking turns to jolly each other up and to count our blessings.

Gradually, and largely without realising it, we started to befriend people. More accurately Alison did. It's her gift to be able to talk to someone for two minutes and come away being their best friend forever. She tells me the secret is that she likes people and is genuinely interested in them. And she is; often she'll know more about a person than they do themselves. While I was content to potter about on my own with a lawnmower, a bonfire or 30 baking potatoes and a tub of oil, Alison did all the hard work of breaking down barriers.

I have always been one of life's observers. Many of the calamities that befall me and trust me there are a few to come in this book, are through inattention because I'm preoccupied watching people. As a child I'd regularly get separated from my mother on shopping expeditions. Sawbridgeworth's[i] lone toy shop became a regular point for us to rendezvous. My exasperated mother would stomp in to find me lost in a world of Lego and model soldiers, bounty which I was informed would never be mine if I kept wandering off. This perplexed me since to the best of my recollection I'd stayed put while she had taken herself off to the shops until somewhere around five full shopping bags later, she discovered that she was alone and had to retrace her steps until she found me.

She tells the tale of leaving me in my pram outside the supermarket and only collecting me when a harassed store clerk disturbed her post-shopping cup of tea by telephoning to ask if the fractious toddler in a pram now squeezed into the storeroom belonged to her? Fifty-three years later she was still cross about her tea getting cold.

Anyway, thanks to Alison's diligence and my ineptitude, ill feelings seemed to pass, and we drifted into the job and got on good terms with our colleagues, helped no doubt by our competency increasing so that we weren't always lagging behind with the bedroom changeovers or merrily mowing the lawn without the lawnmower blade engaged.

We still felt unsettled though; happy enough in our work but something was missing. When we started, we had grand visions of exploring the surrounding countryside in our down time but soon found that we had to force ourselves to get out. When we did, we found some beautiful, quintessentially English countryside and some interesting local towns.

TWO

Darkness on the Edge of Town

The area where we lived and worked was farming country. Large irregular fields with a mix of arable land and livestock, with few public footpaths. Those it did have were often unmarked, blocked by overgrown hedges or deliberately obstructed by the farmers. On one occasion we had to cross an electrified fence that ran straight through the footpath with no protection, stile or other means of crossing other than gingerly climbing under the wire. It added an extra frisson of excitement to our trip but was clearly there to thwart all but the most hardy, acrobatic or stupid ramblers. Back at work I mentioned it to a colleague who suggested I report it to the local council.

At first, I balked at the thought. Was I to become 'one of those people'? Someone who hits middle age and starts complaining about, well everything. My father once objected to a jar of jam on the table at home because it had an advertisement on the label for tights, presumably showing the housewives of middle England that by purchasing a pair they too could look like a supermodel from the waist down. A few weeks later he received a carefully packaged replacement without the offending advertisement. If nothing else, it was an important lesson to me to be alert for this symptom of advancing years and to try and keep my sense of perspective.

Still, I did fill in the requisite on-line form and after a while received a response assuring me that the offending landowner would install some sort of gate. I've no idea if they did but it's nice to know that some council bod stomped over hill and dale to save the ramblers of Staffordshire from mild electrocution.

In truth electric fences caused us little concern. I was a teenager in Suffolk where a group of us would touch them for a dare, occasionally urinate on them and once try to hot wire the fish pond to see if all the fish would pop up, stunned and preferably ready cooked. (They didn't).

One other hazard we encountered on our rambles was the mud. There's a reason why the area is known for its potteries, you could pick up a handful of clinging squelchy clay in a field and fashion a serviceable mug out of it for your picnic. On a walk to the nearby town of Stone we had to negotiate one field where the path across the middle was marked out by a single un-ploughed track. By the time we reached Stone we were nearly two feet taller than when we started out; Alison looked like a 70's glam-rocker in platform shoes.

* * *

Stone is a modest place that despite being the second town in the borough of Stafford (after Stafford), is so unassuming the chances are that you haven't heard of it. There are probably residents of Stone who are uncertain where it is. Even its name means nothing sexier than 'a stone'. Local legend suggests it is named for a pile of stones that marked the graves of princes Ruffin and Wulfad, allegedly killed by their father King Wulfhere of Mercia in AD 665 because of their conversion to Christianity.

It boasts a railway station, was once a major coaching town and nowadays straddles two busy trunk roads and is only a couple of miles from the M6 motorway. Its position on the banks of the River Trent means it has been a stopping point for cargo-carrying vessels since Roman times and held an important position on the Trent and Mersey Canal, the motorway of its day and essential for ferrying pottery safely from the nearby pottery towns around Stoke on Trent.

The canal still boasts the 1772 Grade II listed Star Lock in the centre of town. Once finished it stood for about 24 hours before having to be rebuilt because a cannon fired in celebration of its completion struck the new lock and destroyed most of it. Of all the directions to aim a machine built expressly to destroy property, someone chose to point it towards the nice new lock on which the paint had barely dried.

Nowadays the canal is for leisure, with a big boat yard on the town side of the lock, which supports a rather nice public house, ideal repast after a pleasant tow path ramble, drinkers today blissfully unaware that the building was once a slaughterhouse. Before we leave talk of canals...I met a stout clergyman in Stone whose jumper showed an embroidered logo on his left breast along with the words *anal ministry*, which I took to be a particularly liberal branch of the church until he got up to collect his coffee and I realised that his ample bosom hid the C of Canal Ministry.

* * *

Stone town centre is divided into three distinct parts. The main thoroughfare is pedestrianised and has a pervading sense of hanging on. There are restaurants and shops hiding in narrow alleys, with a few independent stores and cafes that all seem to close early, leaving the ubiquitous Costa to mop up post work/school business. Further down, a cluster of brightly lit takeaways are punctuated by the sort of shops that can't afford a position on the main High Street; a fireplace shop, hairdressers and specialist injury lawyers (or parasitic ambulance chasing evil bastards in the common parlance). The other end of the street a neat triangle of shops and businesses appear more prosperous; a chain pub in the old post office, a fancy tea shop, an outdoor clothing and camping specialist and a few hairdressers of the boutique variety.

On our regular route into Stone was a sad little parade of local shops which included the glorious shrine to cholesterol that is; The Walton Fish Bar.

We called in one day and, affecting the kind of saunter only a southern dandy like me could pull off, I casually leaned on the Formica counter and beckoned a bosomy vison in nylon over and requested two of her finest large fresh fried cod and chips. She held us in her gaze and presumably decided we were a long way from home and needed help.

'I think you'll just need a single chips duck' she replied and scurried off to bellow at someone to prepare them. We then passed a merry half hour helping her remember the name of a song she had stuck in her head that went 'hey hey...'

After about a million fruitless guesses our meal arrived just as we correctly identified her ear-worm - Hey-Ya by Outkast if you're interested.

We got home to unwrap the most enormous portion of chips known to mankind, that burst from a bag made transparent by grease. You could feed a regiment of soldiers on one portion, assuming of course that you weren't too worried about their cholesterol levels.

The portion sizes around this area of the Midlands are a thing to behold; full size sponge cakes cut into four, sandwiches with the cheese filling thicker than the two doorstep slices around it and the local Indian restaurant has a whole section dedicated to 'Belly Busters', platters of spicy carbohydrate and protein of gargantuan proportions.

In spite of its anonymity Stone has given birth to some notable sons and daughters. Among them Eva Morris whose claim to fame was living to be 114, probably by avoiding The Walton Fish Bar, footballer Stan Collymore, Stephen Pyke, who we'll be hearing about later on in our story, and the inventor of Hovis, Richard 'Stoney' Smith, who created the wheatgerm infused bread in Stone. It'll be familiar to those of us of a certain age from the iconic advert featuring a baker's delivery boy on his bicycle negotiating a cobbled hill.

* * *

Stone soon became our go-to place for a pleasant stroll along the canal or a saunter along the High Street in search of bargains. It's a middle of the road town in the middle of the country. It isn't chic and it has no real tourist appeal but it's home to stolid people who have seen its fortunes wax and wane as their local economy wrestles with changing industry and technology.

In many ways Stone represents the underdog, the backbone of the country where people's livelihoods have always been for hire and seldom guaranteed. It is clearly trying hard as a community to cope and to find its place in the post-industrial 21st century.

There are signs that its fortunes could slowly be looking up. There are new, prosperous looking homes being built, the High Street is freshly paved, the tow path and lock are getting a makeover, without artillery pointing at them, new restaurants and wine bars are trying their luck and there's a feeling that spring may be just around the corner.

But if it was, we wouldn't be there to see it. As much as we liked Stone and the area, we had a getaway to plan.

THREE

Where the Streets have no Name

Working at the centre was a treat, a refuge in many ways, for the winter. We learned new skills, felt we contributed to the community and made some great friends. But it was only ever a temporary position and early in 2018 we snuck away for a weekend. Following an online enquiry and a couple of telephone calls we were taking Mavis on an exploratory mission deep into the west of Scotland.

Our first destination though was Strathclyde Country Park, a site run by the Caravan Club, although they have since renamed themselves the Caravan and Motorhome Club in a bold move that incurred the displeasure of traditionalists and the more conservative of their clientele. The message boards on their website were full of unenthusiastic comments about the new logo, the re-branding exercise in general and indiscreet digs at the club. As is usually the case with message boards and website comments the same names keep popping up like passive aggressive moles. After a while I started feeling sorry for them, locked in their own little bubble of insignificance, desperately trying to assert some semblance of control over a scary and unfeeling modern world... well almost, after a couple of minutes in quiet contemplation I decided I couldn't give two hoots about them and left the disenfranchised to their empty threats of boycotts and defection to other clubs.

The journey had taken us from the dull monotony of the M6, through the pass between the Lake District and the Yorkshire Dales and upwards to the border where the English M6 gave way to the Scottish M74 and the landscape changed from verdant greenery to muted greens and russets. It was like the same rain that fed England and made it so lush washed away the colour from the north side of the border.

While Alison drove, I dozed in that undignified way that gentleman of a certain age perfect; snorting, dribbling, guttural grunts and occasional whimpering. I woke in time to casually deflect a string of drool from pooling in my lap just as we were starting the long descent into the outskirts of Glasgow.

To our right ugly tower blocks had been given a makeover, bathed in gentle light and given decorative 'lids' to hide whatever is necessary to plonk on top of a tenement block; water tanks and lift machinery I suppose. I've no idea what they are like inside but however you gild them they will always be the option for those who have little or no choice, columns of humanity stacked on top of each other and placed on the margins, literally and figuratively, of the city. That said I worked with some amazing people who lived in tower blocks in Essex and swore by their community spirit and homely flats, but no amount of fancy paint and concierge services could disguise the menacing atmosphere or negate the need for a suite of back room offices dedicated to maintaining the security of the towers, including a dimly lit room with banks of TVs carefully monitoring every corridor, lift and entrance to the building.

* * *

We were greeted in Strathclyde by a friendly Welsh Warden. I complemented her on her name badge with the new logo on and we were made to feel welcome. It's the little touches that count, like giving us a temporary fob for the gates so we didn't have to go back to her hut and exchange our pitch number for a correctly numbered fob, as we'd be leaving ridiculously early in the morning.

Which was probably just as well because she'd have had a long wait. We were faced with an almost empty site. In theory this gave us a fabulous choice of pitches. In practice we froze, unable to decide. On this chilly evening we eventually elected for a pitch close to the shower block and the 'should-we-drive-front-in-or-reverse-do-we-need-chocks-right-hand-down-a-little-NO-your-other-right-back-a-little-bit-back-a-bit-straighten-up-no-the-other-way-STOP-forward-a-bit-sorry-I-forgot-the-chocks-back-a-bit-maybe-we-should-try-facing-the-other-way-sorry-dear-this-is-fine-do-you-think-we-should-have-filled-up-with-water-first' dance began.

Once we'd remembered where everything was onboard Mavis and had brewed a welcome cuppa, we appraised our options and elected to take refuge in the nearby Toby Carvery. And very fine it was too. Hard to wax lyrical about a chain restaurant but it was reasonably priced, the food was served in generous portions and the staff were attentive and friendly.

Duly sated we waddled back to Mavis and settled in for an early night. Before we went to bed though we were chatting and in response to a rather lame joke we both got a fit of the giggles. Suddenly the tension of the drive, worries about what we might find, whether we were doing the right thing, what our families might think, all our unspoken anxieties exploded out as we wept with laughter, doubled over in painful ecstasy.

* * *

I woke at 4:30am, slightly ahead of the alarm and sufficiently disorientated to forget about the ladder down from our sleeping quarters until somewhere around halfway down gravity reminded me. I managed to land feet first and turn my clumping descent into a nifty pirouette ending at the bathroom with, I suspect, rather less elegance than I imagined.

After braving an early morning shower, we hit the road and the first stop was a 24hr garage to re-fuel. Alison went in to pay and the attendant couldn't have been nicer if he tried, a rare skill at 5am, but even so his demeanour and language were pure Glasgow grit. The accent is harsh, clipped and delivered at a pace even fellow Scots find hard to follow so even a cheery 'have a nice day pal' sounds like a threat.

We took the motorway through Glasgow, busy even at this hour, and into the Trossachs National Park and the joy that is the drive up the western shore of Loch Lomond. As the darkness turned through watery grey into the pale blue of dawn, mountains on the eastern shore loomed out of the early haze and the waters of the loch rippled and shivered in the chilly air.

On the peaks fingers of snow lingered, shaded from the sun in the rivulets and gullies. Below, the land was pale with fallow grass and bronzed with last year's bracken. Rain lashed down spasmodically, driven across the loch by winds, shaking the trees on the bank and giving the road a sheen that reflected the lights of oncoming vehicles. We watched the loch come alive through the soft-focus lens of the windscreen until we turned right at Tarbet, where the road hugged the shoreline and Mavis swung around bends millimetres from overhanging rocks deceptively softened by lichen and moss.

* * *

On we trundled. Sunlight lit up distant hills and mountains while we drove through drizzle. We bounced over roads potholed from the winter freeze and cruised on brand new tarmac, still steaming where neon clad workmen swarmed over dirty yellow trucks laying new carriageway over the old.

After the splendour of Loch Awe and the sparsely populated hills we passed through forest that gave way to open countryside and met Loch Etive. We followed its southern shoreline all the way to Oban. At nearly 20 miles long the loch drains the runoff from the hills and mountains around Glencoe and deposits it into the sea at Connel, where the landscape changed again, and we started seeing signs of more settled habitation; bungalows lined the road and the wilderness gently gave way to the outskirts of Oban. After a hair-raising descent, we rounded a corner and joined Oban's rush hour streets. Despite the snail-paced final mile, we arrived at the ferry terminal in good time.

The ferry crossing from Oban to Mull took 45 minutes and after a light breakfast onboard we took to the windy port deck to catch our first sight of the sombre Duart Castle on its rocky outcrop. (Incidentally port is the left. I'm not sure why nautical coves insist on their own terms for left, right, pointy bit and blunt end but there you go). Once we'd disembarked, we negotiated the single-track A road, turning off onto an unnamed road only slightly wider than Mavis. Moss covered stone walls lined the route, giving way to tumbling grassy slopes and straggly bare trees that allowed tantalising glimpses of the cloudy blue sea and a lonely promontory.

* * *

Our interviews were informal; after a welcome cup of tea and a chat we were shown around and enjoyed scrambling along rough paths and admiring the views. Menacing dark clouds drifted over the open waters towards us and a swirling wind was funnelled between the mountains and hills on either side of the choppy sea. Gulls rode the breeze behind a lone fishing boat that ploughed a silvery channel in the water as it chugged towards the mainland. We took refuge in Mavis as the deluge started and left to our own devices we headed for a campsite overlooking the ferry port at Craignure where we pitched on the edge of the sea looking out over the bay.

We hadn't forgotten our pitching up routine and swung into action, unfurling the electric hook up cable, turning gas on, unpacking essential equipment inside and generally turning Mavis from three and a half tonnes of travelling warehouse into a compact home. It was wonderful to be back onboard. We relaxed and eased into a meditative state, reading and supping tea while lost in our private thoughts about the idea of living and working so far from home and family. Late in the afternoon we looked around Craignure, including a visit to the aforementioned charity shop, walked around the shoreline and cooked our supper. It was all done while batting the pros and cons of working up here between us or mulling them over in the echo chamber of our private thoughts.

As darkness gathered and the lights over the bay and on the mainland twinkled into life we ate and then slid into bed, thankful for the rest after a long and taxing day. We'd just nodded off when the winds that had been gathering all evening started blowing in earnest and Mavis started rocking on her axles. (I'll pause here for you to insert your own smutty joke...)

The Beaufort scale classifies 40mph winds as a fresh gale. We can testify that they were certainly fresh, buffeting Mavis and rattling the fixtures and fittings at irregular intervals and causing her to sway alarmingly. Outside the sea appeared eerily calm, reflecting the swaying yellow lights strung out around the other side of the bay and lapping against the rocky foreshore with a gentle rhythm that was at odds with the squalls pummelling us. We fell into a restless sleep that was punctuated by the sounds of the storm and muffled swearing as we tossed and turned.

* * *

The morning was bright, the wind calmer and the air fresh and salty. We stretched our aching limbs and undertook a cursory inspection that showed Mavis had weathered the storm unharmed. I survived the shower block, rudimentary but efficient and warm, and we took ourselves off to the island's de-facto capital, Tobermory. Fans of the children's TV program Balamory will know it well as it doubles as the eponymous fictional community. It's an endearing place of colourful houses and shops spread around a horseshoe bay. On the drive back, we decided that whatever happened we would return, either to work over the summer or just for a visit, such was the magnificent, rugged beauty of the island.

But before returning to the Midlands and work we had one final challenge to overcome. Upon presenting ourselves for our afternoon ferry back to Oban the nice man in the office informed us that it was cancelled owing to the high winds and waves but the much shorter crossing to Lochaline was running and was making continuous trips to cope with the increased demand.

We queued up for the small ferry, a roll-on roll-off craft which held a handful of cars and vans. We had an hour to wait so we made some soup and discussed again the opportunity before us until our time came to bounce noisily over the steel plates and onto the slick deck, which smelt of diesel and the sea. We rolled over the waves for 20 minutes and into the tiny settlement of Lochaline from where the onward drive took us along the narrow undulating A884, and when I say narrow, I mean single track with passing places and the ever-present threat of meeting a fully loaded logging truck chugging up a hill or hurtling down from the summit seemingly out of control.

And a word here for a local custom that made Alison squeal with delight. To avoid locals having to drag along behind slowcoaches like us the well informed motorhomer uses the passing places to pull in and release them to go about their business at a more urgent pace. One's reward for such good citizenship is a friendly 'toot toot' as the car pulls away. To her delight, Alison collected many toots; I think we got up to around 15 plus a smattering of hazard light flashes by way of gratitude - not as rewarding as a toot but still gratefully received. Only one car just sped grumpily on without acknowledging us. It was an Audi.[ii]

We had one more short ferry crossing to negotiate, across a narrow point on the vast Loch Linnhe, from where we drove into an area familiar to us from previous travels, up through the pass at Glencoe and the bewitching tan wilderness of Rannock Moor with its dark pools of peat-rich waters reflecting the silvery grey sky, and down to skirt Loch Lomond again. Here we swapped driving duties and after seemingly endless driving we eventually pulled up at home somewhere beyond 3am. Too tired to bother about going indoors we wearily climbed into bed in Mavis and immediately fell into a deep and dreamless sleep.

FOUR

Say Hello and Wave Goodbye

Back at work the next morning we still had much to think about, options to weigh up and families and friends to consider, plus we had a house nearby that we hadn't really taken advantage of. Working at a residential conference centre our routines were dictated by bookings, some residential, some day visitors and sometimes both. The variety made it interesting and we met some extraordinary people and learned much more than we ever expected to, but we had found it difficult at times to get away, so our house was little more than a handy place to store belongings and to put visitors up.

We'd finished sorting out our furniture just before Christmas and we'd had a washing machine delivered...on the second attempt. On the first try the driver opened the van, scratched his head and eventually apologised because he'd forgotten to load the washing machine in. Honestly, he had one job to do...

It finally arrived the following morning which gave me an opportunity to swagger around looking faintly butch with a tool kit, although the effect was rather undermined when I used a toilet roll tube as part of my plumbing-in (don't ask).

We thought things over, approached the idea of Mull from every angle, wrote lists and had sleepless nights. It fell to our friend and boss to point out in short, clipped sentences for the woolly headed, 'The opportunity to work on the island of Mull while living in Mavis is as near to the perfect job for you that you're ever going to get so stop messing around, organise yourselves, and go...'

So, we did.

* * *

There's a Laurel and Hardy film where the intrepid duo must deliver a piano up a long flight of stairs. The whole film, from set up to an increasingly improbable series of disasters, along with their continuous bickering, is comedy gold. Of course, for the purchaser of the piano the story wouldn't be so funny...which brings me to our intrepid 'A Man with a Van', who we had chosen to help move furniture out of our house and into storage, partly because of reviews commenting on their friendly service.

At the appointed hour a scruffy white van rattled to a halt outside in a cloud of toxic fumes and dispensed a husband and wife team who, how do I say this politely, would be unlikely to be blown away in a strong wind... or tornado. They both resembled Oliver Hardy, right down to identical moustaches. They eased themselves down out of the van and gingerly set foot on the road in a chorus of oohs and ahs. The gentleman of the duo held his back as he straightened up, something clicked loudly, possibly the suspension on his van, possibly a vertebra, and he shuffled over to us proffering a sweaty palm.

They greeted us like old friends and launched into tales of recent hospitalisation and their collective smorgasbord of ailments, all of which meant that Mr Hardy couldn't lift anything. Slowly this nugget of information percolated through the general conversation and found its way into whatever part of my brain is responsible for registering alarm...whereupon I steered him back to the topic that I felt germane to the situation.

'I'm sorry' I said, interrupting tales of outpatient visits and operations....

'I thought you just said that you couldn't lift?'

It turned out that this was indeed the case. Apparently even showing up in the van was against doctors orders. It occurred to me then that selecting someone to move our heavy items based on friendliness was perhaps an error on my part. Maybe I shouldn't have assumed an ability to lift anything heavier than a donut without dialling 999 was implicit in our contract.

And so, our day spiralled...from eventually getting everything dropped off outside our storage unit by Laurel and Hardy to wrestling the sofa inside while working one floor up on a platform smaller than a double bed. After a few false starts, a twisted arm, a lot of swearing and a few tantrums we realised that it wouldn't fit unless we emptied everything out and started again in the three hours now available to us.

While I panicked Alison calmly negotiated an additional small storage unit to take our extra belongings. We managed a further trip to stuff in more items between bouts of frantic cleaning and during all the comings and goings I had a minor meltdown when I forgot a pin number I needed, and I had to give myself a stern talking to. When we eventually tumbled into bed that night, we had so much adrenaline sloshing about that sleep seemed a million miles away.

Next morning, after an unexpectedly deep and dreamless sleep, we loaded up the car for the first of two runs to the dump, initially with all the usual detritus and household rubbish which Alison was soon having fun sorting into the various bins scattered about the site, while I staggered around with a teetering stack slightly taller than me while trying to work out why every single item required its own receptacle. I remember when the town dump was overseen by surly men in luminous vests and anything short of radioactive waste went into a single stinking skip. At least the Leek site was run by experts in recycling who were not only knowledgeable but charming and helpful too. Our second visit was to deposit some old furniture with a solid heave-ho into what was probably the correct skip, and then fleeing before they discovered that I'd put a cardboard box into the paper bin with malice aforethought.

* * *

Suddenly it was time for goodbyes back at work. I'm not good in such circumstances. I was happy to wave from the window as we went but Alison, who naturally had made friends with everyone, the animals on site and some of the more sociable trees took longer, allowing me time to program the route into the satnav, make a cup of tea, drink a cup of tea, drink Alison's cup of tea and eventually exchange a few shy nods and awkward hugs with colleagues. Last in the line-up were our friends who had taken us in for the winter, offered us work and somewhere to live, who put up with our foibles, guided us, taught us, gave us valuable advice, and indulged us with good grace and kindliness.

By way of thanks we abandoned our cats with them.

The female was just having too much fun adding small squeaky rodents to the endangered species list and Leo, well, Leo was Leo, a saggy bag of loveable attention seeking fur. His confidence had grown considerably, and he patrolled the grounds as if his presence was anything other than ornamental. He did once catch a mouse, probably an old and arthritic one, but none the less his pride was fierce, and he strutted around as if his testicles had grown back, right up to the point where he held his head up so high, he fell off the table.

FIVE

Where Silence Meets the Sea

With goodbyes said we climbed aboard and pointed due north, driving in convoy with Alison piloting Mavis and me following in the car. We would be using Mavis as our home and didn't want to constantly pack up for the journey to work, plus the roads on Mull are mostly single track and narrow so we took the decision to have two vehicles with us.

Left in sole charge of 1.4 litres of thundering Mazda I armed myself with Alison's old Satnav, just in case we got separated. That was how I discovered that she owns the politest satellite navigation system in the world. Instead of the usual assertive instructions, its apologetic female voice suggests routes for you, rather like a timid passenger who knows you're going wrong but is too frightened to challenge the driver directly. Hence every instruction was prefaced with a gentle 'please.'

'Please take a left turn in 300 yards...please turn left now...when it is safe to do so please turn around and take the first right...now really there is no need for that kind of language ...O dear you seemed to have missed it again...slow and steady wins the race...well really, who is a grumpy pants today...'.

And so on. I'm sure if I ended up entangled in a steaming pile of twisted metal in a multi car motorway inferno I'd hear a soothing. 'Oops a daisy, shall I call nanny to kiss it better?'

I may appreciate polite navigational aids, but I don't take kindly towards one of the perils of driving long distances at my time in life, the need for regular comfort breaks, especially so when one has breakfasted on coffee. This trip was no exception and I found myself several vehicles behind Alison and Mavis on the motorway with an increasingly desperate urge to stop when the inevitable happened and the whole carriageway ground to a halt. After an uncomfortable few minutes my attention was drawn to an empty Costa cup in the cup holder. Careful manoeuvring during the infrequent movement of traffic meant that I managed to corral myself front, rear and to my side by articulated lorries, so I seized the moment and put the cup to good use.

I was perched awkwardly recycling the cup and marvelling at the brilliance of my plan when the outside lane started moving and one of Eddie Stobart's fine green trailers slowly became the Crew Alexandra FC Supporters Club bus, a fact I was acutely aware of as I tried to balance a warm brimming cup while...tucking myself in...and desperately trying to retrieve the lid that had somehow rolled into that small corner of the passenger foot well that is tantalisingly out of reach of the driver. While doing so I reflected that at least it wasn't a coach outing of nuns or school children, so I probably wasn't going to end up in court. I gave the Crew supporters a cheery wave as the bus pulled away and mimed sipping from the cup in the desperate hope that they'd not seen what I'd done to fill it.

A few minutes later we were underway in fits and starts and soon rolled into the next services whereupon I carefully scrutinised the car park for signs of the Crew Alexandra bus and, satisfied that it wasn't around. discreetly disposed of the cup and effected my most nonchalant stroll to meet up with Alison who pointed out that my flies were undone.

On we drifted, pulling into the same caravan park at Strathclyde that we'd used on our brief visit to Mull earlier. We ate at the local pub and shared our anxieties about what may lay ahead. Would we like it? What if we didn't? Would we be homesick...and if we were then where was home anyway? We'd sold our old house, spent a season on the road, bought a house in a town that we barely knew and spent most of our winter living at work anyway.

Over something sweet, sticky and totally unnecessary for dessert we hatched an escape plan should it not work out. Which consisted of us handing in our notice and heading back to Leek. Not the most fiendish or original of plans but it felt good having it to fall back on.

* * *

We reached Mull in good time and found our pre-arranged accommodation, a serviced hard standing pitch for Mavis a few miles from work, and we set about transforming her into our home from home.

Outside our window was a lawn fringed with vibrant yellow gorse and beyond a verge peppered with reeds sloping into the grey waters of Loch Don. The tide was in, surrounding the gentle hump of a small gorse studded island that looked like the head of a yellow haired giant emerging from the sea. Across the loch rolling pastures cropped short by sheep rose gently. The landscape was dotted with trees of washed out browns and greens and then capped by the darker hue of managed conifers. Pale rocks poked through grassy hummocks on steep sided hills that were painted from the same faded palette as the trees. Further away murky cloud-capped mountains loomed, teasing us with a sense of wonder and danger.

They formed a rugged backdrop to the gentle sweep of the bay with its boundary of whitewashed bungalows. In places shafts of sunlight broke through the clouds, highlighting features like a spotlight picking out individual players in an orchestra. Here a shimmering silver inlet, there a vibrant rhododendron, now a glade of shrubs with sheep tending to their lambs, a narrow burn of peaty water tumbling down a steep hillside, before the beam moved on and caught us, warming our little patch where we'd parked Mavis for the summer.

As a view it sure beat the basement with a tiny square window looking out onto damp grey steps that we'd just left behind.

SIX

London Calling

O ur first day at work went well. Alison went to work in the shop and got to know almost every customer, which may explain her successful sales figures for day one, and I got to prowl about desperately trying to memorise facts and figures or sit in a kiosk[iii] and sell tickets. Everyone was hospitable, good company and the weather excelled itself by bathing everything in a sunny glow. On the drive home we encountered a herd of red deer, who watched us pass before returning to their grazing. Beyond them the sea sparkled, and the trees stood still and silent, only the chomping of the deer disturbed the peace.

Having completed day one I had to head back to London for a pre-arranged meeting so Tuesday morning we parted company, Alison took up position in the shop and I caught the ferry back to Oban. From Oban it is a dauntingly slow trundle of a train ride through a mountainous landscape. The scenery was amazing though as the little train rolled through glens and hazy mountains. Bluebells basked in the warm sun and translucent bracken shoots poked through the tangle of last year's crop that lay in waves sweeping downhill where winter snow had pressed it. Shimmering lochs and enchanting views appeared from around corners to keep me company on the journey. Also keeping me company was the BO that occasionally wafted over from a party of hikers occupying the seats across the aisle from me.

Despite its remoteness signs of humanity were all around; high deer proof fences protected the railway line, telegraph poles staggered in uneven lines, scarred hills of lonely tree stumps brooded where logging had cleared all but a few scrawny trees, a white cottage nestled snug beside a loch with no obvious means of access, a rusting pipe spanning a remote burn and our train line weaving around road and river as we meandered with slow and steady purpose towards Glasgow.

For all of the beauty outside the window my mind was fluttering from one insignificant topic to another until I closed my eyes and allowed myself to be lulled into a light sleep by the rhythm of the train, only to be snapped back into our rattling carriage by laughter from the smelly hikers or the train pulling into one of the immaculate little stations that line this route. These neat little oases are lovingly tended with crisp flowers, clean swept platforms and are frequently bordered by ornamental gravel.

After passing Loch Lomond we took a left turn to follow the mighty River Clyde towards Glasgow. We swept past market gardens and narrow fields of ponies sandwiched between road and rail. Gradually the landscape became more urbanised until with a grinding of brakes and one last lurch we arrived at Glasgow Queen Street Station. From there I joined the parade of hunched figures marching to the click clack percussion of a dozen wheeled suitcases through the city centre to the majestic Central Station.

According to Smithonian.com:

'The first wheels were not used for transportation. Evidence indicates they were created to serve as potter's wheels around 3500 B.C. in Mesopotamia—300 years before someone figured out to use them for chariots.'[iv]

Why then did it take around 5500 years for some bright spark to stick them on luggage? I ask as someone who has ferried many suitcases around the UK and abroad and come home with biceps the size of basket balls, and a hernia. I've tried carrying them on my back, dragged them until my used underpants are escaping through the worn corners, made my young offspring walk for miles while I stowed the family luggage in their pushchair and conveyed cases by the traditional means of staggering 100 yards, putting them down, shaking my arms, taking a deep breath, rubbing my palms like a weightlifter going for a world record attempt then lifting them, sighing and staggering on for another 100 yards before repeating all over again.

Thankfully these days I can pull my unresisting case behind me into the station, and I was aboard my train for London with time to spare. Nothing could compete with the views I'd already enjoyed so I settled down for hours of reading and preparing for my meeting.

I still get a tinge of excitement as the train lurches through the erratic lights of the London suburbs. I consider myself a Londoner even though I only lived there for the first two years on my life, and again briefly as a teenager. But I love the place and need an occasional fix. Fortunately, I get to visit regularly and immediately fall into the city buzz; the quickened pace, dashing between traffic, grabbing a hurried coffee, ignoring other pedestrians and joy upon joy I get to travel on the London Underground, that glorious fetid pipeline of humanity. I'm secretly a bit of a London Underground nerd, although I guess confessing that in a book rather makes the 'secretly' part of that sentence redundant now.

After nearly 12 hours of travelling I arrived at an anonymous hotel where they favour purple in the décor and took to my room on the 2nd floor. Being a couple of floors up I didn't bother drawing the curtain, which is why a train full of late-night commuters got a cheeky glimpse of middle-aged nipple as their train trundled slowly past my window just as I peeled off my tee shirt.

Breakfast the following morning went true to form. A tomato exploded under my knife and squirted juice and pips over my trousers, I twice had to rescue scrambled egg from the table and my toast was stolen by a Frenchman. Leaving my room, the contents of my rucksack spilled out as I hoisted it onto my back, necessitating an increasingly grumpy re-packing, a scan of the room to check nothing had escaped and then the door slammed behind me while my rucksack sulked on the landing in the path of a departing commuter.

Apologies exchanged I went on my way. Why do we British say sorry when it's patently not our fault...the poor chap had done nothing except be inconvenienced by my luggage, but he politely said sorry and graciously held the lift door for me when I appeared red faced around the corner while still in the process of giving my rucksack a firm talking to.

* * *

The meeting over I wound my merry way back to Euston station where I had an exciting date with The Caledonian Sleeper. Just the name suggests a classic thriller, a sense of glamour mixed with peril; a woman in a glittery cocktail dress slinking along a panelled carriage watched by a bounder in a tux. A retired Colonel will be discovered dead in his berth and the whole mystery will have to be solved before we pull into Glasgow.

Joy upon joy, as I handed my ticket over for my airline style reclining seat the cabin attendant told me that I'd been upgraded to a private cabin due to some technical difficulty. 'But...but...I haven't packed my tuxedo' I pleaded, but Frasier, for that was the name pinned to his breast, assured me that wasn't necessary and bade me bon voyage. Well, along the platform my stoop transformed into the erect swagger of the seasoned traveller whose trunk has been loaded straight from the Bentley and awaits him on board.

I was shown to a narrow little cabin where I took the bottom bunk with its natty foldaway table, concealed reading light and plump pillows. There was a neat little parcel with soap, ear plugs and an eye shade on the bed, which I stowed away as a souvenir like all first-time passengers. I just resisted stuffing the Caledonian Sleeper monogrammed towel into my bag.

A washbasin dispensed water so hot you could make a passable cup of tea with it and directly above, in the exact spot you'd grab when the train took an unexpected lurch while going about your ablutions was the emergency pull cord. With my propensities for vagueness and calamity I decided the safest activity I could indulge in in such a confined space was reading in bed and so settled in with my book and after a short interval flicked off the light and prepared for a good night's sleep.

This proved elusive. Firstly, I'd tried every button and switch, which the cabin had in lavish abundance, to find the correct configuration to extinguish the reading light without summoning assistance, changing the temperature, uncoupling the carriage or putting on the main light. Then as I nestled down, we departed and the train clunked, bounced and shunted out of Euston and all the way to Glasgow in a series of random manoeuvres with no rhythm to lull you into sleep.

Of course, I was also alert for the shrill cry of alarm as the maid found the Colonel slumped over The Times crossword with a knife between the shoulder blades, but I concluded this sort of excitement only happens in first class and with that thought I gradually drifted off.

In the morning as we neared Glasgow, I roused myself, let forth a good trump, and after the American election there really isn't a better term for an explosion of foul gas than that, and took delivery of a cup of coffee and the news that the journey was disappointingly murder free.

* * *

The connecting train to Oban was busy, and soon I took to that dreamy state where your mind wanders into the conversations going on around you. The couple behind me, two mature yet sprightly women, kept up over-lapping monologues that seemed only faintly connected to the same conversation;
'Is that garage red?'
'Aye'
'Ooh. I like that, it's better than blue...'
'Do you like smarties Doris?'
'Maybe. I'm never too sure if I do or not...''
'What do you think of that tree all alone up there?'
'Ooh, so it is'
'Have you been watching that Crimewatch with him off the telly?'
'Och no. I like the green of, what is it now...Oh yes, BP'
'Ooh, did you hear that, Crianlarich next stop; I wonder where that is...'

It was at this point that I leapt over the seats and with a cry of 'be gone from this carriage you foul hags of the banal' hauled them from the train into the loch below to the cheers of my fellow passengers.

Well, obviously I didn't, that would have been impolite, so I just tutted and took solace in recording their conversation in my notebook. I put my ear plugs in, pulled my sleeping mask over my eyes, grabbed my book, sat in puzzled darkness for a few seconds, raised the mask again and set to minding my own business absorbed in my reading. I eventually fell into a fitful sleep until we bumped into Oban.

At around 1:30pm I joined the back packers, day trippers and locals laden with supermarket produce and took the ferry back to Mull.

Alison was working so after an afternoon recuperating, we reunited back at Mavis for a scone and cuppa. We sat outside with tea in hand and birdsong for company. The tide crept silently in, the sun shone and though dinner beckoned we were just too settled to move.

A perfect moment.

* * *

For a mercifully brief period at the beginning of our first season I worked in the gift shop one day a week. Unfortunately, my brain doesn't retain information unless it is hammered in repeatedly for days on end, so one day a week left ample time between shifts for anything I might have learned to leak away.

I made an error on the till with my very first customer. Three postcards at 50p each and I rang through 3 X £1:50. For a moment I stood transfixed, staring at the till, partly amazed at my accidentally accurate if in-opportune mental arithmetic and partly letting the rusting cogs in my cranium clunk and whir towards a solution. Shaking myself from the stupor, I smiled warmly at the poor chap waiting for his change, or so I thought; the way he recoiled suggested I might have looked more hysterical than I imagined. I went through a series of adjustments to the till in a vain and increasingly noisy attempt to get the drawer to ping open. I resorted to hitting mysterious buttons marked [SCN], [X] and [DO NOT PRESS] but nothing worked. In the end I put it through as if three postcards of hairy ginger cows cost the princely sum of £4:50, accepted the £2:00 coin that the poor man had held out for the last five minutes and worked out he needed 50p change. So quite why I gave him three 20 pence pieces is beyond me but anyhow he went away rubbing circulation back into an arm that was numb from holding his £2 coin out for so long.

And so, the long day continued. Alison was working nearby serving in the tearoom and came to my rescue on more than one occasion. Not that other members of staff wouldn't have, but after 18 months of marriage she'd learned to recognise my struggles by the subtle warning signs I display; agitation, weeping, mashing the till keys, throwing things and telling the customer to just F off and take your tartan crap with you....

Okay, not the last one and in fairness the customers are nearly always polite and jovial. The last customer of my first day in the shop cheered me with his Texas drawl and sardonic wit. He was visiting his daughter in Aberdeen who'd just delivered him a new granddaughter. What was so engaging was the way a portly Texan chap, with a belt buckle the size of a toilet seat on his Levi jeans and wearing a moustache that a wulrus would be proud of just swelled up with pride telling me about the new baby. He stood like a denim lighthouse beaming paternal happiness while handing me expensive goods almost at random to ring through the till.

Silence descended as my right index finger moved in slow motion towards the till and hovered above like a hawk scanning for prey. My hand skipped over the keys and rang up a healthy total without apparent error. I smiled and exchanged pleasantries, only marginally spoiling my success when the till drawer sprung open with unnatural force into my groin. I wished him a soprano farewell and slammed the till drawer shut, whereupon it bounced open again with uncanny accuracy.

Alison wasn't without her own tussles. For a while she worked in the tearoom where her biggest challenge, apart from responding to my pathetic pleading, was learning the different combinations of water, coffee and milk that combine in exciting steamy ways to create umpteen varieties of what is essentially a very large or very small cup of coffee.

I'd be hopelessly lost of course, especially since every so often some brat raised on organic WiFi and vegan scatter cushions would ask for a soy latte slow press Nicaraguan fair-trade decaf in a warmed mug and expect a swan to be drawn in foam on the top too.

Alison takes this in her stride, or at least appears to although I was cheered to hear her confess one evening to making a hot chocolate for a customer using a scoop of powder from the jar with the green lid. It was only later that she discovered it was one of two green lidded jars and the other one contained...well actually it contained the hot chocolate, whereas the one she had used was the decaf coffee.

No one complained.

SEVEN

You Brought the Sunshine

It was a strange feeling to be working full time again. On the one hand we were doing a full week as opposed to part time in our last job, on the other hand we had fixed hours, giving us plenty of time to enjoy all that Mull had to offer. On the third hand we got a clean break from work every night, a somewhat elusive luxury when we lived and worked on site. The weather was spoiling us, and we enjoyed views of a loch and mountains from our window or, midges permitting, from the garden.

Mull has many attractions, of which scenery and wildlife feature heavily. It's a must visit if you favour diversions of the natural variety; walking in the hills, historic buildings, ghostly deserted settlements, abundant wildlife and a fascinating history. If your idea of a holiday is whizzy neon, sticky confectionary, STDs and chips with everything then the chances are that Mull won't be high on your agenda.

Driving home from work one evening we paused alongside a campervan to admire a bird floating effortlessly on the breeze. It turned out we got to enjoy a ten-minute display of virtuoso hovering, swooping and general avian aerobatics by a golden eagle. The Dutch couple who owned the camper showed us close ups on their camera, which sported a lens only slightly shorter than its owner, and we all agreed that it was a magical moment. Not just witnessing such a spectacle but being able to pause and enjoy it, to take a break from the routine so that we could experience something special.

Later that week a sea eagle flew over us, lazily beating its massive wings as it drifted across the loch until it became a faint silhouette against a silver sky. The sea, or white-tailed, eagle was reintroduced to Mull a few years ago and is a source of much tourist interest. There is some antipathy from local sheep farmers who blame them (with or without foundation depending upon whom you ask) for taking new-born lambs.

We had previously done what many tourists do and taken a photo of a buzzard thinking it was an eagle. So common is this phenomenon that buzzards are known locally as 'tourist eagles.' I've started referring to sparrows as tourist robins, but it doesn't seem to be catching on.

After only a few weeks of being on Mull we'd seen buzzards, eagles, mink, red deer, all manner of small birds and waders, rock pools full of tadpoles, a newt and a pine martin carrying a rabbit. So far, the supposedly abundant dolphins, whales and basking sharks had eluded us, but I did see a flying fish, although that was only because Alison threw a peppered mackerel at me. We'd found a deserted sandy beach, explored abandoned villages, a stone circle and visited a remote shop that relies solely on an honesty box. Mull is an enchanting place and we had only just scratched the surface.

* * *

Mull is the second largest of the Inner Hebrides. It lays off the west coast of Scotland at the southern end of the line of the Great

Glen fault, which runs from Inverness straight down through Loch Ness and into Loch Linnhe at Fort William then to Duart Bay on Mull.

Mull has around 300 miles (480km) of crinkly coastline and, this is important, it is not to be confused with the Mull of Kintyre, which is a geographical feature at the end of the Kintyre peninsula, on the mainland of Scotland.

The locals are friendly and welcoming. While I was away in London Alison was fostered out to neighbours who fed her and ensured wine flowed freely. We'd taken tea with colleagues, supped beer in convivial company at the local (well, local by Mull standards) and been gifted fresh laid eggs. Island life in a remote settlement relies on a strong sense of community and mutual support. We quickly fell into the local habit of offering a lift to anyone seen walking along the road, which made journeys infinitely more interesting and added a frisson of excitement to a routine trip to or from work.

We were based in a hamlet called Lochdon, which nestles on the shores of, not altogether unsurprisingly, Loch Don, which means Bad Loch, possibly because it is a sea loch that all but drains at low tide. At high tide on days when there is no wind the whole estuary becomes a perfect mirror that reflects the surrounding hills.

The settlement is quite large by Mull standards, nearly 70 dwellings ranging from crofts and farms to cottages, some modern bungalows and a primary school. At the last count 82 souls made up the community, although only 36 of those are Scottish, closely followed by 33 English, 4 Welsh and a smattering of other nationalities to make up the rest[v].

It's an ideal base for us, only a few minutes from Craignure where the delights of the charity shop, an inn, a couple of bars and cafes and a Post Office greet the ferry from the mainland, and we have some great walks from our doorstep.

One of these we tried when, taking advantage of the collision of sunshine with a day off, we took to the hills behind us. The route followed a track up to a cluster of transmitter masts perched on the climb to the summit of Dun da Ghaoithe. The gravel track wound unrelentingly upwards, zig zagging steeply. At one point I believe the brave souls who built it thought to themselves something along the lines of 'bugger this backwards and forwards malarkey let's just go up…' and so they did. Around an innocuous looking corner, we hit a formidable straight stretch that rose unrelentingly upward without pause, sapping our resilience and breath in equal measure.

We paused at the top of this section (in truth we paused many times on the way up) and stood admiring the view while our panting subsided. Rested, we set forth up a further series of switchbacks that brought us to a small cairn hiding behind a compound that contained the masts and various important looking but unguarded satellite dishes, aerials and generators.

From this lofty vantage point we could see Oban on the mainland, the double span bridge at Connel and panning left, mountains too numerous and hard to spell to mention until we found the mighty snow-capped Ben Nevis over 35 miles away which marks the top of Loch Linnhe near Fort William, and the start of the Great Glen.

Below us Lochdon twinkled, we could see where Mavis was parked and Craignure lay hidden below Scallastle forest. Out in the Sound of Mull ferries crossed on their constant duty to keep Mull and more distant isles connected to the mainland. Unperturbed by our aching limbs and developing blisters, or just too stupid to know better, we set off up a gentler track to a further mast. From this point we wandered out over the hill to look down on Loch Spelve, a banana shaped loch fed by a narrow channel to the sea, and out over the Firth of Lorn as far as the island of Jura.

Arresting as the views were the air was decidedly fresher up high and we faced the daunting prospect of slip-sliding back down the gravel track. The rest of the afternoon was spent carefully picking our way down until we eventually rounded the final bend and dropped into a small glen hosting a babbling brook and small farm. We climbed up the other side of the glen and faced a panorama every bit as stunning as the views from the top; Duart Castle in the distance perfectly framed by ancient sun lit oaks and the mountains beyond. It made us appreciate our good fortune at being here on this bewitching island; at least until we started walking again to the now familiar accompaniment of creaking, grunting and the occasional hearty swear.

* * *

I used to be reasonably fit and should have been able to cope with this walk without quite so much fuss, but I now appear to have passed through whatever mysterious portal one falls through to achieve true middle age. Why else would I have nursed blisters and stiff legs for a week, returned to find an invite to the Caravan Club AGM on the doormat, plan any outing further than putting the bins out around lavatory stops, and seem to have a permanent drip on the end of my nose?

The drip may be a legacy of a cold I had been trying to shake off. One of those irritating ones that never quite develops into a fully-grown snot fest but lurks in the background like an annoying tune. I'm not good at being ill, my attitude is generally to ignore whatever ails me until I either recover or get ferried to the doctors. It's an attitude inherited no doubt from my mother, who regarded anything less than a dangling limb a trivial inconvenience to be dealt with by the application of TCP for visible ailments or Rose Hip Syrup for anything else.

When I was young it was fashionable to remove children's tonsils. I'm not quite sure why, maybe there was a lucrative market for pre-pubescent lymphoid tissue in the 60's. Whatever the reason, my mother, a dance teacher by trade, cancelled her lessons and presented me to the Herts and Essex hospital, a collection of dull wartime huts in the shadow of the old Bishops Stortford workhouse, where I was prodded, probed and declared to have a temperature too high for surgery to be safe. I recall little else except being trundled on my bed to the play room and handed a tub of sticky Lego to play with by a bored porter with tattoos and a drooping cigarette behind his ear.

I was kept in overnight just in case whatever ailment I had disappeared in time for bits of my throat to be ripped out the next day. It didn't. My mother appeared fresh from the first bus the next morning telling anyone who'd listen that she'd cancelled her dance classes for the week and therefore 'Raymond must be fine and dandy'. Oddly her diagnosis didn't hold much weight against the collective minds of the NHS, and I was discharged and dragged home with the distinct impression that it was my fault for being ill. The irony of being too unwell to be in hospital escaped me at the time...on reflection it was probably as well that I didn't point this out to my mother.

I did eventually go on to have my tonsils removed, but such was her doubt that my mother kept all her dance classes going that week rather than risk having me running a fever again. On the plus side my father gave me a tiny transistor radio with a crocodile clip aerial and a bakerite earpiece. I discovered the twin joys of music and of drowning out all the background chatter and noise around me. Apart from an occasional passing look at my chart from the nursing staff and trying to work out what was under the nightdress of the girl in the bed opposite, I was left alone with my radio, fed ice cream and was rather disappointed to be discharged at the end of the week.

EIGHT

Last Boat Leaving

History it has been said, is written by the victors. Which is as succinct as it is inaccurate. There are many versions of the same events, as often recorded and re-told from generation to generation by the losers or other observers. Then again there is the precise recording of dates and events that lack any context. It's all very well knowing that the Battle of Trafalgar happened in 1805 but so what? What lead up to it, who was involved, what were the pressures on the war mongers, who opposed it, what was happening with trade, religion, power struggles, how were the ships built, what were the hidden agendas, what role did women play, why 1805, etcetera ad infinitum.

History is a multi-faceted affair and the recording of it is as much driven by a need for brevity and narrative as it is by facts. Inevitably a lot of context gets lost in the recording and depending on the skills, motivations, prejudices and sources available to the writer it'll be slanted in a direction or will favour one version of events. A lot of the research[vi] I have done for this book has been in the form of brief sorties into the busy world of the internet or from reading books.

I tried to read A.F. Murson's book 'King Robert the Bruce'. My goodness it is turgid. First published in 1899 my edition was reissued recently as one of a series of Scottish histories. Of course, A.F. championed accuracy, cross referencing of sources and diligent research whereas I tend to favour frivolity, believing the first thing I read and churning out an interesting diversion and nothing more. Fortunately, there are many other accurate books available, such as John Prebble's excellent trilogy *Culloden, The Highland Clearances* and *Glencoe*[vii]. He is an engaging writer with a narrative flair that keeps you interested in events and people by interjecting some colour and imagination. Real people are given fictional detail, from the drummers blowing on their fingers to warm them before morning reveille to descriptions like this from *Glencoe*:

'His voice was bright, his tongue loose, and although Alasdair's nerves were on edge with distrust, he obeyed his father and made Campbell welcome.'

My point here is that colour and imagination make for good reading. John Prebble didn't know Alasdair's state of mind, whether or not his nerves were on edge, and if so, was it with distrust or indigestion? He made an educated guess at best, but it makes for an engaging read.

My writing is intended for entertainment, with some background for context but it's not an authoritative source. I'm also wont to get distracted, for example, for this chapter I discovered James Puckle, who has nothing to do with our adventures but was just too wonderfully eccentric to overlook.

James Puckle was a lawyer and inventor who in 1718 designed The Puckle Gun, possibly the world's first automatic weapon. It is described (presumably not by him) as clumsy, difficult to aim and ill-suited for warfare. It is unlikely that it ever saw service beyond the test stage. What makes Mr Puckle and his quaint automated killing machine so wonderfully bizarre was its adaptation to be able to fire square bullets.

Why I hear you ask, would it fire square bullets?

Why to kill Muslim's of course I retort, as if that wasn't obvious.

Puckle believed that because square bullets would cause more damage to the victim, they would teach the Muslim Turks the benefits of living under Christian civilization...I'd love to be able to get inside the head that thought that one of the benefits of Christian society was the opportunity to be dispatched in a hail of rounded sanctified ammunition rather than ungodly square munition.

See, how could I leave that out?

* * *

I'm not sure how to follow up an interlude about 18th century racist weapons so just remember, if you want a detailed account of Mull and Scotland's extensive and lively history there are better sources of information than this book.

And so, onto Croggan, gateway to some fascinating Mull history. Croggan is a remote settlement that sits at the tip of a peninsula of corrugated land between the sea and Loch Spelve, a deep water sea loch. Its remote feel is partly due to the effort needed to get there. Historically it would have been accessed by boat but nowadays a single-track road winds its way sluggishly between hill and sea, past jutting rocks and over tumbling burns. In places where it hasn't been patched up rough grass grows down the centre and places to pass other traffic are few and far between. This absence of passing places gives rise to an occasional game of chicken when you come nose to nose with an oncoming car. On most roads here there are plenty of passing points and after a while you learn to time your approach to such a degree that neither party has to slow down significantly.

On our journey to Croggan, having already negotiated sheep, cyclists and geese we had to reverse back over a hillock to let someone pass with the determined and slightly demented look of a local annoyed at finding other traffic on their road. Further on we had to force some ridiculous tank/4X4 hybrid to reverse for a ¼ of a mile. On this occasion we took the high ground, literally, as we crested a bridge and came face to face with them parked up in the middle of the road taking pictures.

After negotiating their rather begrudging reversing we found parking close to the narrow entrance to the loch and walked on around the peninsula, carefully avoiding a young adder slithering across the track, and on to the secluded sandy beach of Port nan Crullach. It was a hot day and we shared the expanse of warm sand with one other family and some sheep. These secluded beaches are all around Mull and are usually empty on even the hottest days.

After a picnic lunch we paddled in warm waters and lazed on the rocks to dry off. Suitably refreshed we set off for our next destination by scrambling up a steep incline through thick undergrowth. The remains of the settlements of Barnashoag and Balgamrie sit in a slight hollow alongside a spring fed burn that tumbles off the cliff in a series of waterfalls and onto the beach below. Or it usually does; the dry spell meant it was just a trickle on that day, making our assent easier. This must have been a tough place to live; isolated, even by Mull standards, the rudimentary stone crofts comprised around 23 buildings and enclosures that were exposed to vicious winter winds and humid midge infested summers.

These settlements were deserted towards the end of the 19th Century, along with many such places in Mull. From the mid-18th Century to the end of the 19th the population on Mull shrunk from around 10,000 people to under 3,000. The Highlands of Scotland and the Western Isles were reduced to one quarter of their population in the same period. Dubbed the Highland Clearances the reasons were far more complex than sometimes reported, and there were several waves of emigration made for different reasons, but the clearances of popular history were essentially the result of greedy out of touch and mostly absentee owners of the land. And I use the word owners in the loosest possible sense. Sometimes the lands were still owned by the traditional Clan Chiefs or their descendants, but more often by absentee landlords who had taken over the lands when they were forfeited after the last Jacobite uprising in 1745; men who were keen to move into polite Edinburgh and London society and 'improve' themselves. They may have believed that they owned vast areas of Scotland, but they were cash poor, relying on their tenants paying a paltry rent via middlemen, or Tackmen, who collected the rents and essentially ran the settlements and oversaw their masters' land.

Then came the sheep. Scrawny local sheep had been a staple of the small holdings but now a hardy Cheviot cross breed that could withstand the harsh winters was introduced and slowly spread south from Sutherland (ironically in North Scotland) in a bleating tide. England was fighting wars, the industrial revolution was underway, and the Empire needed meat and wool. In England a series of Enclosure Acts was creating a 'landless working class' to quote Historian E.P. Thompson, when villages lost common ground to private landowners and often their only recourse was to move to towns and cities where work, albeit low paid and dangerous, was to be found.

To facilitate maximum return the landowners across Scotland, but particularly the Highlands, drove the tenants out to make way for their flocks of sheep, initially using their Tackmen, who imposed impossibly high rents, and sometimes using the militia, and finally the army. There were revolts, but they were largely disorganised. Many of the church ministers, translating for their lords and masters from English into Gaelic, encouraged the populace to move on with threats of eternal damnation, claiming the abundant grasslands of the glens and hills were needed to fulfil God's plans to graze sheep.

The locals were viewed as vulgar, superstitious, idle and incapable of 'improvement' by the establishment. The landowners, or their representatives at least, resorted to the burning of crofts and other harsh treatment. According to contemporary accounts it was often the women who put up most resistance. For example, in one incident at Strathcarron in March 1854 the police force clashed with such ferocity with women blocking their path that their batons were broken on the bonnets of the protesters. There were just two men and a couple of children present to support the women. No injuries to the police ranks were reported but fatalities and life-changing injuries were widely reported among the protesters.

In some places shooting estates eventually replaced sheep, with vast areas given over to grouse, deer, hare and other game, rented out to syndicates of noble gentlemen for their leisure, leading to more clearing of the settlements that remained in the glens.

Then famine struck. Potatoes were a staple in the Highlands and Islands, a cheap crop that would grow in the poor soil, often buried in rows of kelp, and could survive being buried in pits, ready to be dug up in the spring. Potato blight swept through Europe in the 1840s and decimated Ireland from 1845. In 1846 it crept into the Western Highlands and hit its zenith in 1847. Grain was still harvested but was often sent south to keep English stomachs full, causing riots and the intervention of the army. Many Highlanders, already driven to the margins, starved.

Eventually relief came. Some from the landlords but generally through charitable aid from the Lowlands and England. The aid was often dependent upon the people being 'deserving poor' and local ministers had to vouch for the family's standing and good character for them to get any help. Work schemes were introduced to provide labour in return for meagre supplies by some of the more enlightened landlords. The principal form of relief though came in the form of emigration. Highlanders had been emigrating for some time for a variety of reasons but now it gathered momentum. People were encouraged, lied to, forced and all but herded onto any old creaking ship that would transport them to Canada, America or Australia. Promises of a utopian existence were made and people crowded into ships that offered no privacy and often little hope of making the voyage. Many didn't survive the trip as cholera swept through the over-crowed hulls and food and water ran out or was contaminated. Struggling ashore they encountered bleak, harsh conditions and little to sustain them on unfamiliar foreign soil. Many ended up destitute again.

Despite its severe and unforgiving position, we found Barnashoag and Balgmrie enchanting on a sunny day. It is to the credit of the Scots that little settlements like these remain as remote testament to the dispossessed. There are no signs, information boards or even paths, just remote ruins on lonely windswept hilltops looking out over views that few of the villagers would have appreciated in their harsh hand to mouth existence.

It was more spectacular for the effort we'd put in; with no footpaths and the climb up few people had ventured there. We took our time exploring and admiring the views. We went down by a gentler route following what appeared, from the size of the regular deposits, to be deer tracks. I'm not sure what we'd have done if we'd stumbled into a nest of the blighters and accidently trodden on their eggs.

We chanced upon a more complete cottage whose walls were almost intact. It sat next to a burn that tumbled over the rocks in a series of small noisy waterfalls, into a thicket of gorse where a young deer had taken refuge as we approached. Across the stream was a walled animal enclosure and the remnants of old stone walls, one of which we traced downhill.

So liberal are the local laws regarding access to land that in most circumstances you can just wander wherever takes your fancy, so much so that even the Ordinance Survey maps don't show footpaths. That's rather fabulous but it does mean that on occasion one will scramble up a promising ridge to be confronted by an impenetrable deer proof fence with smug looking sheep on the other side and no option but to retrace your steps. We often walk for miles without seeing another soul; it's all quite splendid and makes for exciting escapades.

As we took advantage of the open access land we scrambled over a fence, through a thicket of briars and found the track was on the wrong side of a ditch of bubbling ooze. I secretly wished for a well-trodden footpath and perhaps an information board, toilet facilities and a nice tea shop. Instead we returned to our car which was surrounded by sheep who slunk off with poor grace when we approached.

The sheep certainly took to life on Mull and are still present in huge numbers just about everywhere you look. On the way into work one day we were driving along at a sedate pace and rounded a corner to be confronted by a small flock of them in the road, a not uncommon occurrence here. However, this bunch proceeded to sprint ahead of us on the road, ignoring the lush grass verges and open fields to either side. Clearly seeing their chums having such fun more joined them from the undergrowth until we were surrounded by galloping woolly ruminants. Alison, glancing in the mirror squealed, 'Oh my...I'm about to be overtaken by a sheep...' and sure enough we were. A first for us and it has replaced the Robin Reliant that was Alison's previous personal best in the 'being overtaken by...' competition. In fact, I think it might beat my horse and cart entry. I'll let you be the judge.

NINE

Four Seasons in One Day

Our working life soon settled into a routine; porridge, work, home, a walk if the weather was suitable followed by dinner. The weather was the big variable; we had sunshine while floods occupied England and rain while everywhere else sizzled. The weather is a big talking point on Mull because there is so much of it. The saying here is 'four seasons in one day', but that's maybe two or three seasons fewer than we often experienced in a 24-hour period. We became used to getting wet from pounding rain, leaning at 45 degrees into the wind while getting a tan. Sometimes here, when the wind suddenly ceases people fall flat onto their faces.

It was cold and damp on Mull when I had another London trip to make. Alison was coming with me as far as Oban, so kitted out in head to toe thermal apparel we jumped aboard the ferry and waddled off into town.

Maybe it was the thought of being apart for a couple of days, but things were tense. On reflection it wasn't us, we were as soppy as ever, but it did seem like a day where the irritating and dim witted were out in force. To start with it took 15 minutes to exchange an 8-digit code for my rail ticket. There is no self-service ticket machine at Oban station, so I waited patiently while a 19-year-old representative of Scot Rail with acne and the ghost of a moustache sorted out a railcard for the customer in front of me and explained every nuance of the tickets, seat reservations, direction of travel, stops and the weave of the thread on the seats to someone of equal fastidiousness.

Once his customer had wandered off shuffling his tickets, to the obvious distress of Mr Acne, I took my turn and was proudly flouncing away from his window within two minutes. 'That's how it's done' I said, hopefully in the privacy of my head and not out loud. My display of efficiency was only slightly spoiled by leaving my card in the machine, which I sheepishly retrieved and then I joined Alison in the nearby pub for breakfast.

Having wolfed down a full veggie Scottish breakfast we shuffled to the train in good time, said our goodbyes and I went to board but was blocked by a party of Americans who were genuinely baffled by the luggage rack. How can a country that has put people on the moon and invented liquid cheese create individuals who are unable to stack rectangular suitcases onto horizontal shelves? Once boarded they seemed equally ill at ease with the seat reservations, bickering politely over who would take the window seats and then, half an hour into a three-hour journey two of their number got up to rearrange the luggage. I was privately overjoyed when we jolted into a little station and one of their cases bounced to the floor.

Lulled by the rhythm of the train I drifted off, waking up around Loch Lomond, a not unpleasant place to open one's eyes. Wiping the dribble from my chin I smiled warmly at the lady sitting opposite, a fraternal greeting that was intended to convey apologies for any snoring, belching or farting that my body had enjoyed while my mind was snoozing. We got chatting and I learned about her daughter in Aberdeen, her tortuous journey from Oban and her job as a school secretary. It occurs to me now that that is about all I know. If it had been Alison seated where I was, she'd have names, birthdays, all manner of personal information and have made a lifelong friend. I think it all happens on some other level of consciousness, one that as a mere bloke I am not privy to. It's like being at a concert where I only hear the strings, but Alison hears the whole orchestra.

Having swapped trains at Glasgow I sped south on the comfortable Virgin train. The journey takes almost 5 hours and it's as dull as...well as 5 hours on a train. Alighting onto the grim confines of a remote platform at Euston I dived into the tube and popped up into the sparkly refurbished Tottenham Court Road Station to find that my hotel was spread over two sites, so I had to check into one place then walk back up the road to the other wing. Easy for me but a significant challenge to the poor overseas visitors wandering along looking for a mysterious portal to their room. I pointed them to the entrance and then had to stand impatiently behind them for 20 minutes while they checked in.

When my turn came the staff clearly recognised a veteran globetrotter and waved me through. The façade slipped slightly when I got lost in the maze of doors and signs behind reception and had to retrace my steps to the check-in area. Effecting a nonchalant swagger, I pretended to read the breakfast menu while gathering my wits and set forth for a second attempt. After a short interval I burst through a door, bid the receptionist another cheery hello, pivoted on my heels and, pausing only to wish her an equally merry adieu went off for a third go.

I managed to make it to the fourth floor via the steps before noticing a small sign directing me to the lift. I pressed the button and waited. Every so often the lighted UP arrow would go out and I'd have to start again until I gradually became aware that these instances were accompanied by a ding from somewhere over my shoulder. It dawned on me in a plodding Pavlovian kind of way that the two things were somehow associated; and lo, it came to pass that two further lifts were cleverly concealed behind me. I dived into an open one, waved to the receptionist when it opened on the ground floor, pressed the 9th floor button and waited for what seemed like an eternity before the doors closed on my shame.

My room, when I found it, was comfortable, clean and had a bath. So rare is a proper bath nowadays that I immediately ran one and climbed into what might have looked like a bath but unless you are shorter than 4ft tall was essentially a deep bidet. I had imagined wallowing in mountains of bubbles while eating a crumbly bar of chocolate by candlelight. Instead I sat folded in half in lukewarm water up to my waist under a humming fluorescent bulb and enjoyed 10 minutes of crumpled soapy bliss and five more scrabbling for the towel I'd left out of reach.

* * *

The following morning, I found the breakfast room on the second attempt, the first being thwarted when I got out on the wrong floor. Now, I don't want you think I am ungrateful for what is essentially a free cooked breakfast...but it was awful. Time was when a stale croissant followed by a mountain of carbohydrates sliding around on a greasy plate would set me up for the day. Nowadays I demand slightly more, like recognisable food cooked all the way through, scrambled egg you don't have to slice like rare beef and mushrooms that haven't been left to wilt under the glare of warming lamps for two days. The hash browns looked and tasted like little sponges used to mop up an oil spill. I watched other diners load their plates high and chomp through it all without comment, so I concluded that maybe it was just me.

The coffee was adequate and at least was dispensed quickly without having to select from 142 options.

I returned to my room to collect my bag and check out and like all seasoned travellers searched under the bed, behind the shower curtain and in drawers I knew I hadn't opened just to see if any precious belongings had escaped overnight. Satisfied that they hadn't I bounded down to reception, handed my card in and punched the air with delight at having travelled from my room to the hotel exit in one seamless manoeuvre. Maybe I would wear the smoking jacket for the return journey after all.

In London the outside temperature was so hot it was causing the air conditioning to struggle so I arrived with a sweaty sheen and spent 30 minutes trying to get my various layers off while everyone else effortlessly slipped out of their jackets and went in search of cold refreshment.

I always seem to struggle with simple tasks like getting dressed. The first time I met Alison's son, then a teenager, I went to shake his hand and had somehow zipped both my own hands into my jacket pockets.

If you are wondering how I managed such a feat... so am I.

A tiny part of me wonders if Alison surreptitiously zipped me in so I wouldn't try and ingratiate myself in an embarrassing step-dad-to-be-trying-to-be-cool way by attempting a fist bump then saying something dreadful like. 'Hey Simon, how's it hangin' bro? You lookin' cool dude....' Especially since his name isn't Simon.

* * *

That night, there was be no upgrade on the sleeper train, so I took my place in my reclining seat for the journey. I woke a few times but drifted back off quickly until around 7am when we all staggered off into Glasgow, bedraggled, with erratic hair and pallid yawning faces looking for refreshment and the station restrooms like a zombie invasion that had the foresight to charter a train in good time for the apocalypse.

I was of course early for my connection, skipping through Glasgow's grey dawn and bypassing every breakfast emporium it had to offer, just in case the 10-minute walk to the station somehow meant I'd be late for a train that was scheduled to leave in an hour and 15minutes.

I'm habitually an early person; I will sit in a car park for 30 minutes before a meeting rather than risk being late. I used to build so many scenarios into journey planning that if I followed them to the letter, I'd have to leave a day early just to get to a meeting 45 minutes away. I have reined this in, but I still feel a mounting sense of unease if we aren't sitting in the car at least an hour before a sensible person would be thinking of maybe finishing their coffee and popping to the loo before setting off.

By contrast Alison tends to leave at the exact moment that will afford her the prescribed journey time to reach her destination, with maybe 30 seconds to spare for contingencies. Since leaving office work, I'm much more relaxed and can usually cope but occasionally Alison will wander down in her dressing gown, rubbing sleep from her eyes and discover me showered and dressed, sitting on the sofa like a restless puppy and surrounded by packed bags.

'Morning sweetness,' I'll say while looking pointedly at my watch.

'It's nearly 6am and we need to be there at 11:00. Shall I run you a shower?' I add, in the pointed tones of one who knows that they are skirting with marital discord but just can't help themselves.

Alison will then point out that we're only going to the opticians 15 minutes away and that nothing short of a direct nuclear missile strike would prevent us from being on time. Left to my own devices I'd be sitting on the uncomfortable chair outside the examination room at least 30 minutes early, giving me ample time to read those framed certificates they display to try and impress you.

This is in fact what I did at my last opticians' appointment, which happened to be in a supermarket. They looked very official, neat calligraphy, impressive seal and fancy crest. Only on closer inspection did I discover that Wayne had apparently earned a level 2 certificate in eyeology from Asda University and Lynne had gained a merit in level 1 punctuality. They appeared to be the equivalent of parents sticking young Wayne's 5 metre swimming certificate on the fridge next to the macaroni dinosaur and the sticky magnet proclaiming World's Best Mum.

I wonder if people (normal people I mean, not me) read these things. I assume they are designed to impress at first glance so that you think the spotty teenager entrusted with the future of your eyesight has completed a four year post graduate degree and is now a registered Master of Optometry and therefore safe juggling sharp objects near your retinas.

I suppose that's the price one pays for getting health care from the same place you buy broccoli and crisps. But I went to a proper optician once and the eventual bill for a single pair of spectacles was more than I'd normally spend buying a car...and that was without all the add-on's, tinting, anti-glare, scratch resistant coating, frames, lenses etc. Since then I've trusted my vision to whatever wisdom Wayne and Lynne managed to accumulate on their lunch time seminar. I may go blind but at least I'll be able to afford a white cane and food for the Labrador and while I still have my sight, I can appreciate the framed certificates and numerous signs imploring me to spend money on extras like sunglasses, designer frames or nifty little spectacle maintenance kits.

* * *

While I'm on the subject of signs, there was a sign at work that came back from the printers with a rogue apostrophe. It was up for about half a season before it was corrected. Although I was vaguely aware that it was wrong it didn't bother me, the meaning was clear and if it wasn't for the occasional visitor pointing it out, I'd have ignored it. What I found irritating were the people who felt it necessary to tell me it was incorrect by starting their sentence with 'speaking as...' for example, 'speaking as an ex-teacher...' or 'speaking as a parent of two ...' as if this gave their opinion extra value. I was pointing this very thing out to young Alison when she shivered and told me just how much the sign bothered her. Aside from the more obvious biological differences one of the things that separates me and Alison is our approach to exactness, punctuation being a very good example.

At school I only ever payed sporadic attention to my teachers. My developing brain was reserved for more interesting things like, well like anything that wasn't introduced to me by an adult who was paid to do exactly that. By the age of 10 I could name the Tottenham Hotspur squad, every bar of chocolate available in mainland UK and the members of the Beatles, but ask me to insert a comma into a sentence in the correct place and I'd look at you with rising panic, try and sneak a look at where Simon Gentry on the next desk was placing his and failing that stick it where it looked most aesthetically pleasing.

Unfortunately for me Hertfordshire Education Authority weren't in the habit of awarding points for artistic merit when it came to basic English, and Simon was one of those children who always knew the correct answer and couldn't understand anyone who was struggling. He made a habit of writing with his left arm circling his workbook and his nose 2 cm from the page to thwart me. He once told a teacher it was for 'their own good', meaning me and Andrew Neal who sat the other side of him and who copied Simon's work to such an extent that he once put Simon's name instead of his own at the top of the page.

It's not that I think good punctuation should be avoided or the rules relaxed. My point is about the effect that seeing it has on the individual. Take the errant apostrophe on the sign at work. I walked past it for a couple of weeks and it vaguely dawned on me that something was amiss. After a while I spotted the error, shrugged and went about my business.

Alison on the other hand stopped dead in her tracks the first time her eyes fell upon it, started hyper-ventilating, fanned herself with her pocked Oxford Guide to Grammar, nailed a board over the sign and then got on the phone to me:

'Quick, bring me my correction kit with the industrial size tub of correction fluid, Pantone 1205U, a selection of sable brushes, a ruler, spirit level, plumb line...oh, and best bring the smelling salts lest I suffer an attack of the vapours.'

Okay I exaggerate (slightly) but her reaction is, by her own admission, almost physical. It's not that either response is right or wrong, but as people, indeed as a species, we seem to be divided along our tolerance to imprecision. Hence jazz holds an appeal for me but makes Alison want to claw her own ears off. When writing I quite like an element of chaos from which an idea will coalesce, to be pruned and shaped into something tangible. From there I'll hand it over to Alison who will apply the finishing touches, like grammar, punctuation and accurate spelling.

I think it's the difference in our characters that make us a good team, so long as I remember to put things away and only play my Miles Davis LP's while Alison is out.

TEN

Up on the Hill

After an exhausting day at work we decided to get out in the sun that had finally made an appearance. Thus around 8pm we pointed the car south and drove on a scenic road that loops around Ben More, which at 966m (3,169ft) is the highest mountain and only Munro on the Isle of Mull. We'll return to the topic of Munros later, for now content yourself with the fact that a Munro is a mountain in Scotland with a height over 3,000ft. After turning right at a lonely bus shelter at the head of Loch Scridain we followed the right bank through lonely settlements that hung between the misty sea loch and lush greenery of the lower slopes of the mountains. The air smelled of fresh bracken and sea salt. Wild foxgloves grow on the island and no more so than here where they frame the sea views and colonise the steep slopes that are studded with the deep pink of innumerable plants, all standing straight up like an untidy parade. The foxglove is of course a close relative of the Badgersock and the Otterscarf.[viii]

We swung right and through a mountain pass heavily scarred by logging. Ahead the sky was taking on an amber glow as we drove towards the west coast and the open sea. As the road crested the last hill it revealed the sea bathed in amber under a hazy sun. The island of Inch Kenneth and further out Staffa and the Treshnish Isles were all black, silhouetted against a glow that stretched to the horizon and the air was still and warm. It took our breath away.

Now, before I continue, I must confess that to appreciate this natural splendour we had stopped in a passing space. This is one of the cardinal sins of island life. It's considered to be slightly more serious than high treason and only just below genocide. If the locals have their way it'll become a capital offence. That's certainly the impression gained from reading posts on local forums and listening to the pub chatter. To be fair it is intensely irritating having to reverse for half a mile because some fuckwit in camouflage gear has parked in a passing space after hearing a rumour that a lesser spotted marsh tit warbler is nesting nearby. In our defence we hadn't seen another car in the last half hour and anyway there was ample room to accommodate all but a logging truck in the unlikely event that the Mull rush hour wasn't over.

Moving on from our illicit parking space, the road plunged down in a series of gentle bends to the remote Balmeanach farm and then hugged the shore beneath formidable cliffs along Loch na Keal where we found a remote spot to picnic. It was nearly 9pm and we ate under the golden rays of a low sun while we reflected on our engagement on this day three years before, and the journey we've been on since. The waters of the loch rippled gently, sparkling gold and silver. Opposite us the shores of the Isle of Ulva turned dark as the sun dropped behind the cliffs, occasionally its rays caught us in its beam where glens carved a path through the rocky island. Nothing disturbed the tranquillity of this remote spot; the only sound was the gurgling of a waterfall hidden in the greenery behind us and the occasional contented crunch of a Pringle dunked in taramasalata.

* * *

Driving on in the strange luminescence of the northern twilight we cruised around the loch, through the dappled forests and estate of Knock and up to Salen on the East coast. Here we paused again as the sun melted into the sea in spectacular fashion. We stood looking over ebony shores and a sea shimmering like molten steel. It was a magical display, one of those moments that you must soak in to let the memory burn into your mind; until we were driven away by the midges.

If Scotland is known for anything that cannot be dressed in tartan and sold to tourists, it's midges. We'd only had a couple of days at that point when the little buggers were around in significant numbers, so I guess we did count ourselves lucky. One of those days happened to be when I was alone in my little kiosk selling tickets at work. It was warm and mild, and I had the window shut until a family approached who were performing 'the swatting dance'. This involves walking along at a brisk pace waving your arms about your face and every few paces slapping the back of your neck or cheek, then back to the arm waving. I think it may be the origin of Morris dancing. I had no option but to open the window to serve them and thus my afternoon was spent in the company of approximately seven billion hungry insects.

I'm fortunate in that they don't seem to bite me as much as some people, like poor Alison to whom they are understandably attracted. If you keep moving, they are fine, but stand still and they go up your nose, in your ears and settle on exposed skin. In my little hut that afternoon I experienced all this, plus the added misery of them sticking to the midge repellent I'd sprayed on. By the time I swapped over with my colleague my face looked like I'd spent the afternoon tattooing it. Mind you my replacement was sporting a kilt, so I felt I couldn't complain. I just gave him a sympathetic look and wandered out looking like a Māori version of Pigpen from the Charlie Brown cartoons.

The Highland Midge (Culicoides impunctatus), is one of 35 or so species of tiny flying insects found in Scotland. With a wingspan of just 2 – 3 mm they only emerge in still, humid conditions with low light. They bite, or rather the females do, to get nutrients for their eggs to grow. Until you've experienced them there is nothing that I can write to convey what it is like to experience a swarm, so here are some sobering facts to consider:

· A swarm of them can inflict about 3,000 bites in an hour
· In that same timespan, 40,000 midges can land on an unprotected arm.
· In prime breeding grounds larvae can reach a density of 24 million per hectare (10,000 square metres).
· Legend has it that on the island of Rhum a method of execution was to be stripped naked and tied up for the midges to devour.

* * *

I mentioned Munros earlier. I had heard of them before and thought that along with Corbetts (mountains in Scotland between 2500 and 3000ft high, with at least 500ft of descent on all sides) that about summed up the classification of mountains in the UK.

How wrong that assumption turned out to be. According to one source[ix] there are a bewildering array of ways to catalogue a mountain, hill or lump of rock. These include:

Marilyns, Humps, Tumps, Simms, Dodds, Munros, Munro Tops, Corbetts, Grahams, Donalds, Donald Deweys, Highland Fives, Hewitts, Nuttalls, Deweys, Wainwrights, Birketts, County Tops, SIBs, Irish Simms, Dillons, Vandeleur-Lynams, Arderins and Myrddyn Deweys.

Sir Hugh Thomas Munro started it all. He published his list of mountains over 3,000ft high in Scotland in 1891 and inadvertently or otherwise simultaneously launched hill walking and the naming of any lump of ground slightly higher than a domestic fridge after yourself.

By all accounts he was a fascinating character. Born in London in 1856 he spent a lot of his time in Scotland where he managed and then inherited the family estate of Lindertis. According to Hamish Brown's excellent book Hamish's Mountain Walk, after a spell in South Africa as a young man Munro returned with a collection of curios, antelope heads, a black boy, and a monkey.[x]

I'll let that sink in.

The source for Brown's quote seems to be a letter from one of Munro's sisters, writing after his death. There appear to be no further records concerning the fate of the native boy he brought back as a keepsake of his African adventure.

Sir Hugh never completed his Munros, he died before he could get to the last couple, and he didn't summit on Sgùrr Dearg on the Isle of Skye. This formidable lump is topped by 'the inaccessible pinnacle', a spur of basalt that, despite its name, is regularly climbed by Munro baggers equipped with proper climbing gear.

At time of writing there are 282 Munros. This number changes from time to time thanks to more accurate measurements. The quickest recorded round of all Munros, 39 days, 9 hours, was completed in June 2010 by Stephen Pyke of Stone in Staffordshire; see, I told you that he'd reappear. Just to add to the challenge he cycled and kayaked between Munros.

Hamish Brown completed the first single round (i.e. all in one go) of the Munros in 1974, and the first person to complete, or 'bag' all the known Munros was Reverend A. E. Robertson, in 1901.

ELEVEN

Ride Out in the Country

In the previous chapter I casually let slip that parking in passing spaces on Mull's single-track roads is a faux-pas. What I didn't mention was the correct etiquette when navigating the island by way of its narrow roads. Except for a short lively section of two-lane road between the ferry at Craignure and the settlement of Salen and a few roads around Tobermory it is nearly all single lane, often with grass growing along the middle. We've decided that island drivers can be divided into one of five categories:

Locals

Two local drivers approaching one another will judge the passing space to perfection, requiring the person with the space to swerve lightly around the oncoming vehicle which may, in extreme circumstances require one or both parties to momentarily reduce speed to fewer than three digits. Both drivers will exchange a comradery slight nod of the head.

Commercial vehicles and buses

Even locals find it best to tuck in and wait for the breeze and swaying to subside before venturing on. The driver will give you a half-hearted thanks by raising his hand while staring straight ahead. They will be followed by a procession of cars and vans, all of whom have resisted any opportunities to pass, because following one guarantees safe and speedy passage.

Regular visitors

Some think of themselves as locals because they visit once a year in the family Mondeo to see a buzzard that they swear is an eagle and to chat to that nice man in the ferry office. Many of them drive about as if they own the place, randomly pull into passing spaces to look for otters and are impossible to predict. One moment they will pull over in good time, the next they are distracted by a waterfall and merrily plough on, forcing you to screech to a halt and reverse around a corner and halfway up a mountain. When they pass, they'll give you a cheery wave that resonates with smug do-goodiness and too much Daily Mail.

Newcomers

You can always tell someone new to island driving. They're the ones sitting in passing spaces weeping. They spend their first day hopping from space to space, sometimes sending their children on ahead to scout out the road. They pull over as soon as they see another vehicle, even if it's on a different island. Occasionally they pull over into spaces on the opposite side of the road rather than risk the oncoming car not doing so. When you pass, they sit like a nervous puppy waiting to find out if they've been a good boy or a naughty doggie and if you raise a hand in thanks they beam with pathetic gratitude.

Late for the ferry

These are people of indeterminate pedigree, but they share the same desire to reach the ferry in time, whatever the cost. They will just keep driving at you, irrespective of where the passing spaces are. They seem oblivious, stupid or too arrogant to realise the system works perfectly well if all parties play by the same rules. We've been forced into narrow roadside gullies, soggy verges and hedges by people rushing towards us like they are in the outside lane of the M25. They studiously avoid eye contact and the only acknowledgement they get from us involves one or maybe two fingers.

Audi drivers

Anyone familiar with Downwardly Mobile will know how loathsome we found the behaviour of many Audi drivers. Well, we're here to testify that on Mull they have been universally courteous and polite.

There, you didn't expect that did you?

* * *

After a fractious encounter with a tit in a delivery van we decided to recover a little on the tranquil island of Iona. Sitting off the west coast of Mull, Iona is a 10-minute ferry trip and another world away. It's surprising to find an island only three miles long by one mile wide so busy, with tarmacked streets, shops, a pub and a post office. But then there has been a settlement on Iona for centuries owing to its place as the root of Christianity in Scotland and quite probably (sources vary) into England and throughout mainland Europe.

It all started in 563AD when an Irish monk called Columba (later to become St. Columba) left home under a bit of a cloud. After upsetting the owner of a gospel he'd copied in his native Ireland he then went against the King's ruling and refused to hand the duplicate over. It all sounds a bit like playground pettiness but somehow this squabble descended into a bloody mess that became known as 'The Battle of the Book' and claimed 3000 casualties.

Columba scarpered, supposedly full of remorse and chose Iona as it was the first place that he set foot on where he couldn't see his native Ireland. He established a monastic community and set about converting pagan Scotland and Northern England to the Christian faith. Iona Abbey became a missionary centre and place of learning known throughout the world and turned this dot of sand, rock and wind into a place of pilgrimage.

St. Columba is the focus of much adulation and pilgrims still visit to venerate him and soak up the atmosphere. However, he wasn't without his eccentricities. For example, he banished women and cows from the island, claiming that 'where there is a cow there is a woman, and where there is a woman there is mischief'.

He is also said to have buried his friend Oran alive in the foundations of the Abbey.[xi]

The Abbey was particularly known for the illuminated manuscripts the monks produced there. This was where 'The book of Kells' was produced in around 800 AD, perhaps the finest medieval illuminated manuscript ever produced. It's something of a miracle that it survived; many manuscripts were destroyed in successive Viking raids. Despite murders and looting the raiders failed to destroy the spirit of the island and the Christian community continued. Kings and Saints are buried on the island, as is John Smith the late Labour Party leader, whose simple headstone we searched for, but we gave up when the rain started seeping through our coats.

Iona is also home to the original Celtic Cross. The arms fell off the first stone cross made there, so some bright spark added the iconic circle around the intersection of the horizontal and vertical beams as a device for supporting the arms.

To those who believe such things, Iona is known as a 'thin place'. By which they mean a place where the earthly world and spirit world is close and some of the mysterious and spiritual realm seeps through, although it might just mean porous if the amount of rain we encountered is anything to go by.

I was just about to clamber up a small hillock where it's said St. Columba had his writing shed, and could presumably look out for bovine or female interlopers, when a startlingly loud clap of thunder persuaded me that a cynic standing out in the open on high ground at a holy site in a storm was bound to attract lightening. 'Ooh, we never have storms on Iona' said a passer-by as I slithered down the slope, contrary to the evidence lashing down on her from the black clouds above. Her face was briefly illuminated by lightning and we both paused as the crack of thunder followed almost immediately.

I shrugged and we squelched off to seek refuge in the Abbey.

* * *

The original Abbey is long gone, replaced in 1203 by a nunnery for the splendidly titled Order of the Black Nuns. After the Reformation it lay in ruins until 1899 when its restoration began. Today it's a simple building of stone and damp. There are ferns growing high up on the inside walls, but its simplicity is also its charm; a large, gentle nave, hushed cloisters and a tiny chapel on the site where it's believed St. Columba is buried. I confess to a perverse pleasure in knowing that around 50% of the visitors paying their respects are women; I hope the odd cow pops by too to say, 'hi, no hard feelings about the banishment'.

The occupants of the Abbey nowadays are a Christian community who believe in action as much as prayer and reflection. There was information about the plight of refugees, Palestinians, people living with HIV and support for the LGBT community available, so I helped myself to a handful of pamphlets, which I later found fused together in a soggy ball in my coat pocket.

We had a peek into the gift shop and tiny but interesting museum and then scurried through the rain to catch the evening Eucharist service at the nearby Bishops House, a Christian retreat house that isn't affiliated to the Abbey. It was a short, good humoured service which we followed by a discrete nose around and wandered back to catch the last ferry home. On-board we agreed that we'd barely touched the surface of Iona and vowed to return when we had more time and Iona had less rain.

Two years later we still haven't been back.

TWELVE

My Ever-Changing Moods

The week after visiting Iona we ignored all our experience and took ourselves on a walk of nearly 12 miles over rough terrain, in hot weather and for which we were ill prepared, to see the Carsaig Arches, a pair of natural arches carved out of the cliffs by the sea.

Carsaig itself is little more than the remnants of a large estate, once owned by the Macleans of Pennycross. It sits in a pleasant cove with a small stone pier and little else that we could see, although I am sure that there is more to it if you explore a bit. The journey there was spectacular, through a wooded area then down the side of a steep sided valley and into the small car park. We were cheered to pass a lonely red telephone box halfway down the descent which had a minor role in the 1945 film *'I know Where I'm going.'*

Buoyed up by the drive and the sunshine we set off along the beach and into a narrow strip of vegetation and boulders that sat snuggly between the cliffs and beach. The walk wound along goat tracks (the area is well known for its feral goats) and under cliffs crowned with basalt columns.

The track was steep in places, we had to divert over landslips and across the beach at times until we paused for lunch on a shingle spit, in sight of a tumbling waterfall, one of several on-route. For two hours we saw no one until we neared our destination where two grim faced couples passed us on their return journey. Despite her best efforts Alison only managed to illicit a grudging good afternoon by a stout chap clad in ill-fitting walking attire. We wondered what we'd let ourselves in for.

Eventually we finally scrambled up around Malcom's Point, site of the bleakest and most remote ruined cottage I've ever seen, and up to the point from which the first arch is visible. A sea arch, as I'm sure you are aware, is caused by wave action eroding a cliff. The one at Durdle Dor in Dorset is magnificent. This one was magnificently underwhelming. Maybe it was the long trek, and the fact that experienced walkers though we are we are also human and therefore prone to what one may charitably call idiocy. We were under supplied with water and let ourselves be deceived into thinking the sun wasn't strong because of the breeze. We sat and pondered the return journey, ate some peanuts until I helpfully spilled them, and then set out for home.

It was a long, trying trudge back. Occasionally a seal would bob up a few yards out to sea and watch us, possibly contemplating how tasty we'd be when we eventually expired on the lonely beach. We passed many goats munching seaweed, and of course the scenery was every bit as glorious as it had been when we set out in the morning, but by now we weren't in the mood to appreciate it. The final part of the walk along the beach and up a short path was a relief, but the greatest joy was to discover that our stash of chocolate ginger biscuits hadn't melted in the car. We sat in crumbly silence savouring every bite before finally rousing ourselves for the drive home, which was enlivened by sight of an impressively antlered red deer stag crossing the road ahead of us.

* * *

Back in Mavis I took up the local magazine as a distraction from my aching limbs. It's a cheerfully amateur affair packed with information from small ads, what's on listings, local news and reports from various local organisations, all the knowledge essential to keep island life ticking over. It's an important and entertaining publication for islanders and for those wishing to keeping touch with Mull from further afield.

They publish letters to the editor too, and if you have ever read a local paper, you'll know what an absolute delight letters to the editor can be. Immediately one caught my eye, so I made a cup of tea, grabbed my notebook and warned Alison that I was warming up for some curmudgeonness.

A chappie by the name of Adrian Derry,[xii] a visitor to the island from North Yorkshire, wrote to complain about insensitive developments and intrusive signs spoiling the island. On the face of it this may not sound unreasonable, but then Mr Derry rather undermined his argument by the examples he chose to illustrate his points.

For a start he objected to the signs warning that otters may be crossing the road. I quote.

'The otter is one of my favourite mammals but, as with all of Britain, you get road kill.'

Firstly, it had never occurred to me to have a favourite mammal, although thinking about it I suppose I do rate humans somewhat higher than, say antelopes or Nigel Farage[xiii]. Secondly if it is your favourite Mr Derry why then would you object to a discreet warning sign? They are just standard red bordered triangles with a silhouette of one of your favourite mammals on after all. Hardly intrusive.

Then Moy Castle came in for his ire for allowing banners promoting the Heritage Lottery Fund. If the option is to receive valuable funding to save an historic monument at the cost of a little advertising or to let the castle crumble, then personally I'd choose the banner. I've been to Moy Castle and the signs are discreetly placed on a nearby fence. The Mr Derrys of this world seem to expect the planet to be as he wants it irrespective of real-life considerations and compromises.

Getting into his stride he started on self-catering lodges and a brand-new restaurant building. Frankly a few log cabins are hardly offensive in the grand scheme of things and the new building may not be everyone's cup of tea, but it is well designed, provides jobs and brings in money to the community. Mull relies on tourism, there is only so much forestry, fish farming and livestock the island can sustain, and the otter community just won't pay their fair share of taxes, probably because they keep getting squished by their fans.

Mull is a working community, with all the detritus that may entail. If Mr Derry wants a pristine holiday destination without having to encounter real life, then I'd suggest Disneyland is a better option for him. Or Mars. I'll contribute to the cost if it keeps him away from Mull.

Our Adrian finishes with what I suspect he thought was a clever flourish:

'As I've said, the powers that be no doubt mean well, but I think they should look up the meaning of the word 'aesthetics' as soon as possible and put it into practice?' (The question mark was all his own work).

I assume he means 'concerned with beauty or the appreciation of beauty.' as the online Oxford Dictionary defines it. Like the beauty to be found in the rays of the early morning sun reflecting on an otter's guts smeared across the road or the appreciation of the empty homes and boarded up shops as people leave to find employment on the mainland. Or maybe the appreciation of a society that isn't some Disneyfied plastic facsimile but a real living, breathing community that has jobs, welcomes tourists, protects its wildlife and could benefit from the addition of a sign or two warning of narrow-minded idiots from North Yorkshire.

The odd angry letter in the local magazine is nothing though compared to local social media. Mostly it is useful titbits of information, notices and events but from time to time an innocent posting will attract the attention of a few keyboard warriors.

For a while it seemed that you could put the date on the page and people would disagree with it, until the admin for the group tightened up the rules. Nevertheless, frank exchanges of opinion do crop up and the one that seems to stir up most emotion is the rather vexed subject of motorhomes.

Now of course I must declare an interest; we live in one and it is wonderful, we spent a lot of time on the road in it,[xiv] so I am biased. I'm not going to re-hash the arguments here because if my experience of social media has taught me anything it is that my opinion will make precisely no difference at all.

However, for the purposes of balance let me offer two thoughts on the matter, one from each perspective:

1   Motorhomers–If you deposit your waste and chemical toilets in watercourses, under bushes or indeed anywhere not designated for such a purpose you should be repeatedly dunked in a tank of your own effluent.

2   Locals–When complaining about motorhomes slowing down your commute, if your stream of vitriol starts with 'I've lived on Mull for 12 years...' the only correct response is 'Then you should know better by now then shouldn't you and leave earlier.'

On the plus side most of the posts are delightfully positive. Requests for picking up parcels from the mainland are a regular; people popping over on the ferry will cheerfully collect packages, even prescriptions, for strangers. I've seen requests for the 'loan' of some medication until the recipient's supply comes in, odd jobs needed, lifts and rooms for the night and the charmingly obscure such as:

'Does anyone happen to have a spare ¾" gear cog for a Tohatsu 50HP outboard motor knocking about? I can pay you in duck eggs or I've a wicker hamper and half a tub of Vaseline I no longer need.'

It's all refreshingly old fashioned and trusting in a positive way. Unlike some places that revel in their 'Merry Olde England' ways Mull's character is stolid and realistic. People rely on each other and share a mutual trust that comes from all being in the same position. One day it could well be you needing a prescription picked up by another islander, so it pays to invest in a little neighbourliness.

Plus of course we get otter warning signs, interesting buildings, looked after castles and the opportunity to piss off Adrian Derry of North Yorkshire into the bargain.

THIRTEEN

Tillidh Mi
(I Will Return)

id you know that the Scots Gaelic for tyre is taidheir? I know this because our car was sporting a dinky little space saving tyre. (Dinky mòran rùm sàbhaladh taidheir[xv]) We'd had a persistent steering wobble and when we eventually checked it out, it turned out that we were about ½ mile away from our tyre exploding in a vigorous shower of sparks and rubber. At first, I thought that the mechanic had mixed our Mazda up with a wheelbarrow, but apparently the space saving tyre was safe and legal so off we scooted at a pace unlikely to trouble the speedometer. The mechanic found a replacement for us and had it shipped over in a few days. I'm guessing from the cost it had its own private cabin on the ferry from Oban and made ample use of the mini bar.

There is a resurgence of Gaelic speaking in Scotland, no more so than in the Hebrides where an estimated 52% of the population speak some Scots Gaelic. There's a Gaelic TV channel, a Gaelic Language (Scotland) Act 2005 and announcements on the ferries are in both English and Gaelic. Scots Gaelic, is a Celtic language brought over from Ireland in the 5 and 6th centuries that has developed into a language of its own. Its influence doesn't stop at Scotland's border though; for example the words whisky, brogue and trousers are all from Scots Gaelic. And where would we be without trousers?

Well, Scotland probably, or at least The Highlands and Islands as they often favoured the Plaid, a basic woollen blanket of up to four metres in length, usually woven in a local pattern. ('Pladjer' is Gaelic for blanket). This was pleated and secured around the waist with a belt and then fixed over the shoulder or worn as a hood, as well as serving as a handy blanket at night. From this emerged the kilt[xvi], a more recent invention that is essentially a pleated skirt sometimes worn with an ornamental sash which represents the over the shoulder element of the plaid. According to some sources the flashes that wearers of kilts use to hold their socks up are a hangover from the cords that were once tied below the knee to keep one's skin-tight leg coverings, or triubhas, in place. Truis or trews are the Anglicised spellings, hence we arrive at trousers.

Contrary to popular myth Highlanders often wore both a plaid and trews, especially in inclement weather, of which Scotland is abundantly blessed.

A lot of what we think of as Highland culture doesn't come from the Gaelic speaking natives. For example they might well have worn a practical plaid, coloured according to the supply of local plants to make the dyes, and patterned by local weavers, but tartan as we know it today, along with all the impractical adornments like bejewelled dirks (daggers worn on the kilt belt), sashes and ridiculous hats were an invention hawked in no small part by well-heeled gentlemen of dubious Scottish legacy, the ruling landowners of high society who romanticised the Highland life.

They formed groups like The Society of True Highlanders and The Celtic Society of Edinburgh in the early 1800's to peddle a fashionable faux nostalgia for all things Scottish, to celebrate the very heritage that they were eradicating by their greed. One-time President of the Celtic Society was Sir Walter Scott (author of Rob Roy & Ivanho) who managed to get King George IV north of the border, the first foray into Scottish territory by an English monarch for 200 years. It was Scott and his assistant David Stewart who assigned official tartans to each clan, sometimes creating entirely new ones, seemingly out of thin air. This may not have been as cynical as it sounds.

Following the Battle of Culloden in 1746 an Act of Parliament was passed which made the wearing of tartan a penal offence. Although a register of tartans was kept in Edinburgh, over time the details of some patterns and colours were lost and old tartans perished, leaving limited evidence for Scott and Stewart to work with, at least for some of the smaller Clans.

Along with the banning of tartan the Gaelic language was outlawed following Culloden, which makes its resurgence more meaningful for many people, especially, but not exclusively, in the Scottish Independence movement. Whatever your political thoughts on the subject it is a beautiful language to listen to, gentle and melodic.

* * *

One of the other things I like about Gaelic is its ability to make the mundane sound mysterious and romantic. For example, the highest peak on Mull, A' Bheinn Mhòr now mostly goes under the dull but easier to pronounce moniker Ben More (Big Hill). My attempts at pronouncing the nearby abandoned settlement of Gualachaolish required Alison to shield herself with a sturdy umbrella. Its Gaelic meaning is 'hill shoulder at the strait' which is far more manageable, and so it turned out to be when we took a walk there.

The route took us a short drive out of Lochdon then a long walk up a track that was slowly losing its battle with nature, across open grassland and around hills. It was in regular use until the 1930s when the last crofter living at Gualachaolish left. Our guidebook warned us the way was boggy and indeed the path regularly sank into fetid pools or became an improvised stream. Even as we gained higher ground, we were forced to seek alternative routes to avoid bubbling springs and muddy puddles. After a half hour ascent, we reached a gate and the end of the track. From here on it was footpath only and the way became more interesting, with bracken and fern fighting with wild foxgloves for supremacy, lonely trees bent with the wind and strips of shrubs tracing the route of dark peaty burns running off the hills. As we climbed, the view behind us opened to reveal the plain of the river Allt a' Ghleannain that feeds into Lochdon and out over low hills to the Duart peninsula with the castle silhouetted against the light blue of the sea, and beyond to the hills of Morvern on the mainland.

Heading onwards we traced Loch Spelve as it narrowed towards its entrance, sandwiched between the hills we were on and those overlooking the remote settlement of Croggan.

As we rounded the edge of the highest point on the peninsular, we started dropping into a lush valley with a burn running through the remains of a stone animal enclosure. As we walked on more and more stone ruins became apparent amongst the bracken and the hills were criss-crossed by gently tumbling stone walls. Below us lay the ruins of Killean church, once an important stop on the pilgrimage route to Iona when pilgrims alighted at nearby Grasspoint and made their way west through Mull.

Fording the burn, we made our way on to the croft at Gualachaolish. In the mid-18th Century, the house was lived in by a

Mr W. Middleton, Factor to Colonel Campbell of Possil, who once owned great swathes of this part of Mull. The position was magnificent, overlooking Croggan, Loch Spelve and the sun-drenched waters of the Firth of Lorne and mainland Scotland beyond. It's doubtful that the Factor would have had much free time to enjoy the views, but I like to think he'd have been joined by his family at the end of a long summers day, all of them sitting on the wall looking out over the sea and sharing a moment of stillness in the warm summer air, just as we did.

* * *

Mr. Middleton appears to have been a well read and erudite gentleman if his testimony to the Poor Law Enquiry of Scotland in 1844 is anything to go by. It's worth noting though that his witness statement was in a 'Memorandum of Conversation' and there is no way to evaluate the accuracy of his testimony, nor to assume that his willingness to advocate emigration as the only recourse for poor crofters in his charge was his own opinion. While it might have been true, and I've no reason to doubt it, sheep, as previously mentioned, were much more profitable than people to a landowner and emigration was sometimes engineered so that it was the only realistic option left. When Middleton states that some of the crofters were behind with their rent one must remember that some Factors, acting on the landowners' orders, set unreasonably high rents deliberately to drive locals out. He does though talk about the help they were given to emigrate, and his testimony suggests that the landowner, Colonel Campbell of Possil, was more benevolent than many.

Whatever his opinions the remains of his croft sit in a stunning location and enjoy an air of peace and solitude. The well-trodden path suggested that people visit the area, but to the credit of the occasional visitors there was no rubbish or other outward signs of their presence.

We climbed up the hill behind the croft and looked down on the small overgrown graveyard at Killean church then started back, around the ruins, back across the burn and up around Carn Ban. Far below the occasional car shimmered in the afternoon heat as it sped along the road and behind us a small sailing boat drifted into Loch Spelve and navigated around the fish farm that bobbed on the clear waters. We walked gradually downhill to the plain and back to the car pondering on the lives of the people living here in times gone by, when subsistence was hand to mouth and generations of loyalty brought scant reward beyond the opportunity to sail from your ancestral home to foreign soil, never again to tread these hills, to listen to the burn tumble over the stones, to smell the heather and bracken and never to look out over the loch and sea to familiar mountains.

> *'Free were the fields of fern*
> *Free was the fishing in the coves of care*
> *Empty are the homes of old*
> *Empty for the sake of summer's cause*
> *Yes, you're taking it all away*
> *The music, the tongue and the old refrains*
> *You're coming here to play*
> *And you're pulling the roots from a dying age.'*

Waiting for the Wheel to Turn, Highland Poem 1747

FOURTEEN

These Days Are Mine

It was a sunny day at work. The rush for entry had died down and had been replaced by the ambient noise of people lazily enjoying some rare sunshine. The air was still, hazy with the sweet smell of freshly mown grass mixed with the tang of the sea. Somewhere over the hill a mower was purring, the shouts and cries of children mingled with bird song. Families bickered and laughed, a lad playing football with his friends provided a running commentary on his own prowess, a toddler crunched over the gravel and picked up a handful to fling, just for the delight of the texture; bored teenagers moped along behind their parents. Walkers stomped around in expensive boots and trousers with too many pockets, discarded layers of clothing flapping from backpacks like ragged flags.

A young couple leaned into each other awkwardly as they sat together on the grass and tore at a shrink-wrapped picnic. They both ducked as a swallow swept over them, laughing together as they re-assembled their al-fresco lunch, perhaps their first as a couple. Away in the carpark a dog bounded free of captivity, excited children tumbled out of the back as their parents unfolded from the front, the father placed his hands on his hips as he arced his back, stretched out and straightened up with an approving nod as he took in the views. The sea was motionless, mountains blue and hazy, topped with fluffy white clouds like piped meringue.

Two pensioners ignored the view, and passing the young couple they smiled, maybe remembering when they too were young lovers having their first picnic, a rare interlude in busy lives, rations saved up for a corned beef sandwich wrapped in tissue paper and a boiled egg each, washed down with a flask of hot, sweet tea. Distant memories that fade in the sun.

* * *

The day flowed on with its own rhythm; the early rush, families awake since first light trying to occupy restless children, then waves of visitors as the ferries come and go, the lunch time lull, the afternoon walkers and the post Iona trip hustle as people try to squeeze one last attraction in before they dash off to catch the ferry back.

My colleague came to replace me in the kiosk. I rose from my raised seat, frozen in mid crouch and slowly toppled sideways, flinging an arm out to brace against the wall just in time. Ninety minutes of sitting on a stool and my right leg had taken the unilateral decision to go to sleep without any prior notice or permission from the rest of me. This is a problem I usually only experience at night.

Climbing up our ladder to bed is a wonderful feeling. I know that within minutes I'll be startling myself back into consciousness by dropping my book, at which point I'll exchange a goodnight kiss with Alison, turn onto my side, snuggle down, close my eyes, get up to have a wee, bump into the table, repeat the whole exercise and then discover that despite over 50 years of close acquaintance with my arms they suddenly get in the way. Whichever way I lay I seem to have a spare limb and can find no way to lay without it causing me grief. Surely after a few million years of evolution we'd have developed a way to fall asleep without ones left arm turning into a nocturnal speed bump.

Worse still is the experience of waking to find a completely useless appendage beside you because it's numb from pins and needles. At times I've had to lift one arm with the other just to move it out of the way. Occasionally I'll turn over and a whole arm that is only notionally attached to my body will thrash across Alison without any conscious effort on my part. By careful honing of my husbandly instincts I usually manage to convey the impression of a loving hug, although she's less enamoured when my supposed tender embrace bounces off her nose.

* * *

While the good weather lasted we realised that we needed to take advantage of the sunshine and arranged a jaunt onto mainland Scotland to meet up with friends. We rendezvoused at Callander, a small homely looking town on the river Teith that is used as the fictional Tannochbrae in the Dr Finlay's Casebook TV series. The town sits beneath steep cliffs with trees clinging on to seemingly impossible slopes. The cliffs mark the Highland Boundary Fault, through which Bracklin Falls tumble and where we soon alighted for a pleasant stroll with our friends.

First stop was at one of the friendliest cafes we've visited. Access was through a clothing store and upstairs to a light and airy seating area. Walking up the stairs I was slightly tense from holding back my natural inclination to bolt up steps two at a time.

I don't know where this stems from but faced with any flight of stairs I will habitually zip up them. I've often turned to talk to Alison at the top of a stairwell and found myself alone and out of breath. Alison meanwhile will be walking up like any other sane person with that look of quiet bewilderment she reserves for such occasions.

In the days when I had a proper job where words like heuristics and synergy featured without irony I was suited and booted at a meeting in swanky offices overlooking the British Library in London. After making awkward small talk with the people I was there to meet we headed for the stairs where I leapt off with my usual gay abandon, only to find myself alone on the third floor. Ten minutes later I found them looking baffled and slightly worried by my sudden departure. Evidently, they had all used the elevator then spent the rest of the time looking for me. I noticed that for the return trip I was discreetly rounded up and herded into the lift.

Anyway, the reason for climbing the stairs in Callander was that the café was dog friendly, ideal since our friends had their pooch with them. Not only was he made welcome with a bed and choice of water bowls, but a waiter directed him towards a tin of dog treats. On reflection I now feel slightly cheated by this; why was I not directed towards a tin of cakes and choice of relaxing seating rather than a menu and one of those chairs that is just about comfortable for 20 minutes until your bottom goes numb?

Which is a trivial observation as the food was very good, the service attentive but not over the top and the company delightful.

After a ramble to Bracklin Falls we popped in to see Doune Castle. The castle features in one of the most notable moments in world history, the filming of Monty Python and the Holy Grail (MPATHG). I found the Monty Python TV series rather hit and miss but MPATHG was in an entirely different league. It was of course silly but for all its irreverence it presented medieval history in a more realistic way than sanitised Hollywood nonsense where the actors are suspiciously well groomed and the damsel in distress has found time for a hair-do and managed to slap half the Avon catalogue onto her perfectly lit face before allowing herself to be rescued[xvii]. I'll save further analysis because after all it was just a daft film, but I loved it and took great delight looking at the places where iconic scenes were filmed.

We didn't have time to go inside so I missed where sir Galahad was rescued from administering spankings to the bathing maidens, a scene that I paid meticulous attention to as a teenager. We did however see where the French guard utters the immortal lines, 'I fart in your general direction! Your mother was a hamster, and your father smelt of elderberries!', so I went away happy.

After Doune we called into an antique centre where a café awaited our patronage, but not until we'd wandered around the stalls. I tend to stay clear of these places nowadays since I've noticed an increasing amount of the items on sale I not only remember but, in some cases, still use. I have underwear older than some of the antiques we looked at. Today though melancholy thoughts were impossible as our little party sat down to tea and cake outside in the sunshine and drizzle in true stoic Scottish fashion, following which we went our separate ways. It was all too brief, and lovely though they were, Callander, Bracklin and Doune were just pleasant backdrops for a day spent in first-rate company.

Our day out also served to remind us of one of the drawbacks to our lifestyle. Making new friends and acquaintances is one thing, Alison is very good at it and I'm quite adept at trailing along in her wake, but for all the new relationships we make nothing can replace the depth that comes with long standing friendships, bonds that have weathered the years and ridden the storms, friends who will instinctively be there beside us when we need them, just because we need them. It's those people we parted from who we now have occasion to miss.

Technology makes the world smaller nowadays, conversations can happen instantly on a mobile phone where once they required a trudge to a distant phone box, a stack of coins and a willingness to shut yourself in a booth smelling of stale tobacco and urine. Well, at least that was my experience of trying to keep in touch with friends while I drifted aimlessly around north London to escape the damp room that I shared with a colleague.

I don't have any friends from my school days, whereas Alison seems to be friends with most of her classmates from her mother's pre-natal maternity classes onwards. But that's fine, we are wired differently and have different needs; that's one of the reasons we are together. On Mull, we've found a network of people who are warm and supportive and who have welcomed us to this island and into its community, even though we arrived in a motorhome.

* * *

At the beginning of this chapter I described, in a somewhat flamboyant way, a sunny day at work. True to form since that day it rained almost continuously. Mull enjoys, and I realise that's a debatable term, around 4500mm (177 inches) of rain a year. In an average year it rains somewhere on Mull for 283 days. That's...well that's a lot of rain. It is windy too, which combines to create horizontal precipitation of a curiously penetrative nature. Mull does have one trick up its geographical sleeve though. Due to the mountainous nature of its centre the weather can be very local. It's not unknown for us to leave home in fine weather and arrive five minutes later at work in driving rain. While we're battening down the hatches our neighbours back in Lochdon will be slathering on the sun cream and wondering if 10am is too early for a G&T.

We don't let the weather spoil it though. Thanks to the Gulf Stream the climate is mild and on a day off we can usually head for a part of the island that isn't half submerged. On one such jaunt we took ourselves to the north of Mull to walk up to Crater Loch which, as you've probably guessed, is a loch in the crater of an extinct volcano. It's about 60 million years since its last eruption so we felt reasonably safe. We were able to walk around the rim and enjoy spectacular views across the northern end of the island while speculating on the possibilities of the cone being hollowed out and used as the lair of a supervillain. My instinct is to now write a background about the conditions that created it, but geology has its own language in which words like denudation and diagenesis feature heavily. At the time I was working my way through a book on the geology of Mull and Iona that was intended for 'the layman and interested amateur geologist'.

I think that was the last sentence that I understood.

In contrast many of the walking guides to Mull are delightfully vague, written by enthusiastic amateurs and in whose hands precision and detail take a back seat to flowery descriptions and the assumption that you instinctively understand, for example, how far to walk uphill before the turn on the left by the big rock that you have to pass if you want to avoid becoming a red splash on the beach far below.

The fact that since it was written landmarks like gates and trees have been replaced, moved or rotted away is a detail too precise to trouble the author. At least the route suggested in our guide book was simple enough, even though it advised us to start from a place that doesn't exist.

On our return journey we passed a family group cycling their merry way along the narrow undulating road. We see a lot of cyclists here on Mull enjoying the fresh air and healthy exercise. Actually, I very much suspect none of them are enjoying themselves if only they'd admit it.

They are inevitably led by a father who last mounted a bicycle when he was 15 years and five stone younger. The kids just wanted to go to Centre-Parcs and think cycling is boring, Mull is boring, mum and dad are boring and if dad points out one more sodding eagle, they'll insert it where its beak will make that saddle he keeps moaning about even less comfortable. Meanwhile mum is wondering why she's ended up carrying three rucksacks and how she let herself be talked into this nonsense when Portugal was cheaper, hotter, flatter and had inexpensive wine on tap.

Older children and family holidays don't always mix but we were fortunate to have my two adult children visit for a couple of days and they gave a good impression of people enjoying wall to wall wind and rain. We picked them up from a station just outside Glasgow after they'd fallen for the local trick of sitting on the portion of the train that doesn't leave the station. They eventually arrived and we promptly got stuck in traffic thanks to my navigational skills. Once clear of Glasgow's motorway madness we proceeded to fling them around every tight bend on the road to Oban to make up time and catch the ferry.

Which we did with minutes to spare. After the rush we relaxed onboard and headed into a glorious golden sunset as we sailed over to Mull, with plumes of cotton-wool cloud rising like smoke from the peaks. Back on the island we introduced them to some of the delights that Mull has to offer, including, 17 different types of rain and a walk to the abandoned settlement of Shiaba where we narrowly avoided stepping on a rather disgruntled Adder.

It was a brief interlude before we were back at work and my two boarded the ferry to make their way home by boat, train and plane.

However old they are, however grown up, children are our most precious gift; brief lives in the cycle of the universe that we nurture and give to the world where we hope they'll make a difference, live contented lives and leave the earth a tiny bit better off than when they arrived.

FIFTEEN

One Fine Day

Towards the tail end of our first season when the wind blew it carried the crisp tang of chilly evenings and days warmed by the shortening sun. Shadows lengthened noticeably earlier every evening and we had clear nights under a canopy of stars. The smudge of the Milky Way arching across the loch and fading into the hills is a remarkable sight, especially for two people raised under the sodium glare of streetlights. The trees turning were a marvel too. Evergreens erect and almost glowing while around them others turned russet, rich copper or gold.

It also marked the slightly weird time when holiday makers cannot reach a consensus on what constitutes correct holiday attire. We were treated to the spectacle of robust couples of a certain age rustling up the road in more layers than needed for an attempt on Everest, while behind them were families wearing shorts and tee shirts. I witnessed someone smear sun-cream on their arms and face then throw on a waterproof coat and hat, all for a two-minute walk back to her car. I suspect some of the shorts and tee shirt brigade were determined to wear them because they were on their holidays and no amount of wind or rain would deter them.

This was generally my father's approach, a simple formula:

Holiday = Shorts.

Thus, on our first morning at some out of season shack on the Norfolk coast he'd appear in baggy shorts with two unnaturally white legs dangling out like pieces of knotted string tucked into sturdy boots. My mother would pause from scrubbing the chalk outline that marked the last resting place of the cabin's previous inhabitant and say something soothing and supportive, like, 'Oh, for goodness sake Donald, put those away, you'll scare the children'.

Her application of the second syllable to his name should have served as a warning, and in normal circumstances would have, but he was on holiday and therefore ignored her and led us out to whatever diversions one could find on a deserted beach in November. Generally, this meant putting the windbreak up, an activity that should have earned him a fortune as the inventor of hang-gliding. Sometimes he would glide gently along the sand behind it, other times a gust would lift him up, and deposit him a few yards further up the beach wrapped in poles and cloth. Once he'd located his glasses, shaken the sand from his shorts, tripped over a pole and been pinched by a crab he'd shout back to us, 'this seems like a nice spot'

We'd trudge up to find it was indeed a fine position for watching the sewage overflow pipe, which may just be better than the bloated corpse of a seal I was busy poking with driftwood or the other family we passed who, I was reliably informed by my mother, must be a bit weird because who in their right minds would come to Norfolk in November for a beach holiday?

We never ventured far from home for family holidays, but my mother let it be known that she had once visited Scotland for a holiday. I'm assuming it was on purpose although if she oversaw navigation one can't be too sure. I didn't know that my parents had ever visited Scotland but thanks to my sister I found out that they holidayed in Oban, a town we've grown familiar with as our gateway to Mull.

In fact, they took the train to Oban and as they passed through Gretna Green my farther proposed. I found this peculiarly touching. My father was a nervous chap and I'm sure he must have worried himself to distraction over the arrangements and whether she'd say yes. My mother was a practical soul and wasn't blessed with a romantic leaning so I can't imagine how she would have responded. Did he get down on one knee and if he did, did the train lurch round a bend flinging him sideways? Did she just say yes, or something like, 'for goodness sake Donald, get up, the carpet's filthy'?

Were they more romantic, touchy-feely than when I invaded their world a few years later?

Why don't I know these things?

Because they never told me, and I never asked.

I grew up, grew away and seldom thought of them as human beings with pasts, hopes, dreams, desires or...well...as anything other than as parents.

I know now how selfish that is.

In the case of my mother I've come to realise that part of her resistance to acknowledging feelings, hers and others, comes from a place I'll never get to know or understand. As she became increasingly frail and her memory seemed more comfortable in the past, I got to know her better. Better than I ever did through all the years I spent with her as I grew up, left home, had children of my own and visited her as an adult. Better perhaps than I could have ever expected to.

But I never quite understood her. Something niggled away at me every time I left her after a good chin-wag over a cup of lukewarm tea and a rich tea biscuit in her nursing home.

We'd laugh, she'd tell us tales from her youth, from school, as an evacuee, as a young woman in London, as a TB patient and about her mother the dressmaker and her father and his affairs and dalliances around Tottenham.

I came to understand, or more accurately Alison did, that what troubled me was the veil she'd drawn over some periods of her early life. As she aged, so the defences she'd built up over a lifetime became vulnerable to her drifting memory. A darkness would gather from the edges of her smile and with eyes focused on somewhere we couldn't see, she'd drift away.

Moments later she would snap back again, making a joke or re-telling a funny story; but for a moment some malevolent spirit seemed to hover just out of our sight.

Doors long closed creaked and had to be locked shut again.

I've no right to intrude on her past, and it may be just imagination on my part anyway, but my sadness is that she may never have dealt with her demons, that they have haunted her for so long that their presence has become almost reassuring.

It troubled me that evening as I looked from our little idyll on Mull towards Oban that I never really understood my mother. I blamed her for a lot of things, some unfairly and others, well, harshly perhaps.

SIXTEEN

Living on The Edge

It had been a long season and what we needed was some quiet time to reflect and wander, without work or domestic chores to intrude. So, at 5:30am on a surprisingly sunny day a rather startled Alison responded to my perky, 'good morning sunshine, fancy a trip to Lismore?' with a brisk and somewhat indelicate reply.

She rallied magnificently though, and by 7am we were safely aboard our first ferry and heading to Oban. The 2nd leg, from Oban to Achnacroish on Lismore took another 50 minutes aboard a ferry of compact charm, a single roll on-roll-off car deck, full today of trade vans conveying such necessities as plumbers, electricians, carpenters and food to the small island.

We took up residence in a cabin that smelled of oil and saltwater, along with a young couple from Belgium and a charming and slightly eccentric Scots/Canadian couple, now residents of Toronto. We were clad in walking gear with waterproofs in reserve, as were our continental friends. The Canadians though wore designer shoes, expensive clothes, and he was in shirt, tie and jacket. We'd arranged to return by the same ferry later while they were heading up the island, on foot, in the hope of securing a lift to the other ferry at the top end of the island. Further investigation revealed that they had to be in Glasgow for a late afternoon meeting and would therefore need to find swift transport to the ferry...on an island of 190 people and few cars.

Having done our homework we knew the scenic route to the island's heritage centre, so immediately took a track that soon became a boggy path. As we were skipping from rock to rock over a particularly gruelling section of field where the locals appeared to be cultivating mud I glanced back and saw our well-dressed friends from the boat following us.

'I hope you know where you're going?' he called in a cheery Canadian drawl as he balanced one exquisite cowboy boot on a tuft of grass while he dislodged the other from a patch of bog.

I reassured him that we did, but only after a brief consultation with Alison, whose wise council I've come to rely upon in matters of social interaction, so I neglected to add that in fact the road from the ferry would have led them directly to the heritage centre with nothing more challenging underfoot than the occasional pot hole. As Alison put it, this was a much more interesting route and they'd get to see some of the lovely countryside, even if they didn't want to.

We eventually emerged at a remote cottage serviced by a lane that would lead us to the heritage centre past a loch of almost bewitching banality. I think we'd become rather spoilt for fine views so this loch, while not at all unpleasant, was just rather so so.

We arrived 30 minutes before anything was due to open, so we sat in the sunshine to enjoy the view...or at least looked at the view. Somehow on an island barely one mile wide and surrounded by mountains and stunning vistas, they'd built their museum and café on the one spot with nothing more interesting to see than a road and a couple of rough fields. Even the rather dull loch we'd passed would have been more diverting.

I've since discovered that the land was in fact donated to the centre which of course makes my jibe about the views seem rather mean spirited, especially as once inside the museum was incredibly interesting, thoughtfully laid out and easily accessible to all, from the casual visitor to the ardent historian. It also housed a perky little gift shop selling local books and crafts and was home to a Gaelic library. Even more cheerily it had an excellent café that we took advantage of. Our chums managed to purchase a few souvenirs including a book about the island and a £200 painting, and then ended up getting a lift to their next ferry with the author of the book they'd just bought; such is life on a small island.

* * *

One of the interesting nuggets of information we picked up in the museum was the story of St. Moluag. It seems that at one time he rivalled St. Columba of Iona for ecclesiastical supremacy in the winning converts league table (West Highland Division 1). He founded a cathedral on Lismore before sailing around the western isles and on to Iceland, presumably because he had been called up for an international fixture. The cathedral's chancel is now Lismore parish church.

According to legend Moluag even won a coracle boat race to Lismore, defeating Columba by the unusual but apparently effective method of cutting off a finger and throwing it over Columba and onto the island, thus being the first to touch it and claim victory. Columba rowed away in a bit of a huff, uttering distinctly un-Christian curses at the victor, like: 'May you have the jagged ridges for your pathway."

Which seems a trifle mean spirited and surely earned him a holy yellow card. Despite Columba's hex, for a while Lismore rivalled Iona as the seat of Christian learning and evangelism in Scotland, but Columba had the one thing Moluag didn't; a biographer to secure his place in history at the top of the table, leaving poor Moluag fighting to stay out of the ecclesiastical relegation zone.

Anyhow, I'm sure there was a lot more to it than that, but we'd got to that point where we needed to strike out for pastures new or risk missing the ferry. Thus, we walked up the road, zigzagged down an unsigned steep side track and emerged at the remains of Castle Coeffin. Well, what a splendid spot. The ivy covered remains sit on a stump of twisted rich green rocky pasture. Next to it is a small inlet with a shallow beach where at low tide a medieval fish trap is exposed. It was a remote and bewitching place, charming, slightly spooky and wonderfully remote.

After capering around the castle for a while we wandered back along the road, popped into the heritage centre to avail ourselves of their lavatories and have a peer into the reconstructed cottage showing how life was back at the turn of the 19th century. Pretty sparse by all appearances but at least your cottage came with a fire extinguisher and Perspex leaflet holder.

Wandering along a road isn't everyone's idea of a fun day out, and indeed it isn't usually ours but the combination of sunshine, wild flowers (the name Lismore comes from the Gaelic for great garden), mountain views on all sides and bird song was intoxicating. We strolled past the shop/post office/public-noticeboard/cottage, listened to someone checking volume levels in the public hall that also doubles as the Doctor's Surgery, probably not at the same time, although inviting an audience in to witness Flora Bloggs getting her ulcers dressed or young Thomas having his vaccinations probably passes for entertainment on a remote island.

On we went, took a left turn and descended along the road that took us back to Achnacroish, with its neat little primary school and an enterprising chip van doing a roaring trade serving the tradespeople waiting for the ferry home. We met up with the Belgium couple and a host of others gathering to catch the boat. There was no sign of the Canadians, so we assume that they either made it to the other ferry or were detained by the locals and made to work in the mud fields until they'd learned how to dress appropriately.

* * *

On returning to Oban we discovered that CalMac, the company operating the ferries, had, in a masterpiece of timetable planning, managed to arrange our ferry's arrival at Oban at precisely the same time as the Mull ferry left just 20 yards away. Although there may well be complicated scheduling reasons for arranging it like that it was very annoying.

We then discovered that the ferry departure lounge had been colonised by the England Formation Shuffling and Shouting Team (senior division). They queued quite unnecessarily for 45 minutes despite ample seating being provided, the whole time carrying on conversations that would drown out a jet fighter taking off. They all appeared to have been sponsored by Edinburgh Woollen Mill, except for one ruddy chap who sported a Red Sox baseball cap, Craghoppers walking trousers, Adidas shirt and Niké colostomy bag.

Of course, once we were called to board everyone else had to wait as the narrow gangway was blocked by loud septuagenarians in pastel leisurewear desperately trying to shuffle in front of each other. I seriously considered hijacking the ferry and setting a course for Switzerland and was wondering if I could get a good group rate at Digitas until Alison reminded me that Switzerland is completely landlocked, and anyway we'd be trapped with them for far too long. Even the 45 minutes to Mull seemed like a lifetime when they took to circling the ferry in little flocks and pointing out the obvious to each other.

'Ooh look, there's the town...'

'See that Jim? That's the fish farm...no wait no it isn't, it's a lighthouse...'

'Do you remember when we were here last Doris?'

'No...'

'Nor do I....'

One of them peeled away from their display of close-formation wandering to report some lost property; I suspect it might have been marbles.

Rather than risk getting caught up in their meanderings we avoided the cafeteria onboard so I rummaged around in my rucksack and discovered that my refreshing drink, of the sparkling cola plant variety, had survived the day but now lay vibrating with effervescent malevolence in my rucksack. I tried gently twisting the cap and a hiss of steam escaped, so I carefully set it aside and furtively helped myself to Alison's bottle of water instead.

I still think of fizzy drinks as a luxury. We never had them at home when I was growing up. When I complained about the unjustness of being denied tooth rotting gassy refreshment my enterprising mother would (I'm not making this up) add a spoonful of Andrews Liver Salts to my orange squash to make it fizzy. For the uninitiated, Andrews Liver Salts was, and indeed still is, a laxative and antacid that comes in powder form.

Added to squash it sent lively bubbles up my nose and left a chalky white film on top of my drink. How I envied my friends with their Panda Pop colas and Fanta orange moustaches.

Mind you, Alison reminded me that I once tried to make Champagne by putting white wine into a Sodastream, with predictably disastrous results. I still think it's a genius idea that just needs some fine tuning when I get the time...

With a bump and much excited muttering we arrived back on Mull and having secreted my bottle of rumbling fizz into the luggage of a member of the England Formation Shuffling and Shouting Team I hurried Alison down the gangway before it went critical.[xviii]

SEVENTEEN

Sing to My Soul

As the nights drew further in the soundtrack to our evenings became the bellowing of the red deer stags. They roar to display dominance and gather together a harem of hinds. They fight with their antlers to see off interlopers while they 'service' between 30 and 40 hinds, to borrow a phrase from a rather polite source I found online.

It all sounds jolly musky and masculine, two prize specimens battling for mating rights in a cloud of testosterone. An illusion that was rather dispelled by the roaring stag we interrupted on our way home from work who gave us a camp shrug and pranced off in the manner of a My Little Pony dressage competitor at a Pride gymkhana.

Being light on their feet is an impressive attribute of deer, who can wander through woodlands with barely a sound, whereas in my efforts to take pictures of them I trample through as if the entire undergrowth is made of exploding bubble wrap.

Hearing and sometimes seeing them was a reminder that at the beginning of the season the land was dry, the air warm and hazy and the hazards while out walking were minimal. After a summer of rain rambling became an adventure fraught with risks and perils, mostly of the wet and squelchy kind. Such was our experience hiking through Glenforsa. The glen is a broad valley with a sparkling river and is flanked on both sides by wooded slopes and rugged hills that funnel the glen to the foot of Beinn Talaidh, a prominent mountain at the heart of the island.

First though we had to get 'togged up' in the correct attire for such a venture. Alison slipped her walking gear on with effortless grace while I skated over the gravel carpark only to find I was wearing my coat backwards. Alison gently helped me out and we set off.

When I started getting serious about hiking, more serious than taking the dog for a walk to the pub via the long route anyway, I equipped myself with all manner of hi-tech walking attire designed to fool the overweight desk jockey that I was into believing that I was God's gift to mountaineering and that scaling any peak higher than a mole hill counted as serious climbing.

One of my purchases was a coat. It was bright red, had more pockets than I could possibly use and plenty of zips in unlikely places. The salesman promised that it would keep me snug in arctic temperatures and cool under tropical skies. Which it did, if you accept that the nearest it ever came to arctic conditions in suburban Essex was a cool breeze and if the weather was balmy, I didn't wear it. But the most disturbing thing about it was that it came with an owner's manual. I've purchased cars with less information than what was apparently required to master a nylon skin to cover the upper half of my pallid body.

One evening, bathed in the yellow glare of a hotel reading lamp, I prepared for its first adventure by digesting the manual. In the morning I was planning go boldly where only 3 million people every year fear to tread, and climb (walk up the footpath of) Kinder Scout in the Peak District. Apparently, my new coat had a snug pocket for a homing beacon in case of avalanche - I put my chewing gum in it, a map pocket that was too small for my OS Routefinder, a hood with three different types of fastener and many other adornments that I seldom used and some I never found. The material was designed to survive all but the most extreme of temperatures, would wick away sweat and it even had little zipped vents under each armpit to let the stink out, although I think the manual put it more delicately. One whole chapter was dedicated to laundry instructions, which I skipped over. After 30 minutes of struggling with all manner of jargon and erroneous nonsense I binned the manual.

It was a good coat, I felt rugged and vaguely like I knew what I was doing, although I was undoubtedly wrong on both counts. Nevertheless, it served me well and was eventually replaced by a succession of cheaper models after one too many laundry mishaps. Yes, I know I should have read that chapter.

Recently I tried the specialised expensive coat route again. This time, since my job entails much outdoor work in everything the west coast of Scotland can throw at me, almost all of it wet and cold, I went for a long wax jacket designed for cowboys and stockmen who spend their time herding cattle and corralling wild horses.

I should have known better.

For a start it reaches down to exactly 10" above my wellingtons, meaning that I come back inside dry as a bone except for a soggy band just below my knees. Secondly, it has a built-in cape that I assume is meant to keep water from cascading down my neck. This does seem to work, but at a price because it's fastened by straps that reach under each arm. This makes putting it on an adventure that invariably ends up with me twirling around chasing a limp sleeve flapping about tantalisingly out of reach, or I'll cut off all circulation to an arm because its wrapped around so tight. Fortunately, unlike cowboys on the prairie I have Alison who will hear the tell-tale crashes and swearing and come to my rescue, check that I have my mittens on, spit on her hanky and remove flecks of breakfast from my chin and warn me not to play with the rough boys from the estate.

But the biggest flaw in a product explicitly designed to deal with wet and windy conditions is the metal fasteners that hold the collar and hood in place. Left to their own devices they whip about in the slightest breeze and leave angry red welts down both of my cheeks. Doing the top one up prevents this from happening but has the unfortunate side effect of cutting off the blood supply to my head.

It does have the redeeming feature of leg straps that you can step into to stop the tail flying around, although when I tried them, they made me walk like a toddler who'd had an 'accident' in the underwear department. I'm told that these also mean that you can wear it while riding a horse, but that's an extremely unlikely scenario. Still, it's nice to know that I have something in my wardrobe that could pass muster as bona-fide outdoor wear from a shop that doesn't have a permanent sale or too many letter X's in its name.

A thought I comforted myself with as our route took us along two miles of track that was pleasant enough for a walk but with every step our destination became more menacing. True to form the local guide book suggested that its assent would be suitable for an afternoon stroll with granny and a couple of toddlers. To us the 'nose' of Beinn Talaidh appeared almost vertical and the carpet of cloud so confidently predicted to depart by early afternoon sat on top like a sulking child sent to sit on the stairs to think about what they said about Aunt Doris's wig.

We ploughed on towards the bothy at the foot of the climb up but after a tussle with a raging torrent of white-water rapids, or gentle burn if you were reading the same guide book as us, we turned back. We decided to strike out instead for the lower hills and chose some that lined one side of the glen that we'd walked in on, our intention being to cut down a handy slope to meet the track about half way back.

We soon found ourselves struggling up a hill of springy reeds and crossing swamps on 'stepping stone' tufts of grass and woody plants that may be a wild herb or some endangered species of local flora. If it is then it may be considerably more endangered since our trek – sorry.

We made heavy work of the lower climb but as the slope grew steeper, so the ground became firmer and we reached the peak, took in the view and plunged on. To afford some shelter from the breeze we followed an animal track below the ridge that slowly but surely descended towards the glen. Faced with a boggy patch I heard a shriek accompanied by a watery squelch and muffled swearing from behind. I took a moment to compose myself before turning around and sloshing to Alison's aid, some sixth sense telling me that a huge grin wouldn't brighten her day at that precise moment.

Restored to the vertical and with only a few muddy patches to show for her intimate acquaintance with the hill we trampled on, splish-splashing through quagmires and spongy grasses for 400 yards or so, until a high decibel assault on the frailties of the Scottish landscape from close behind me was cut off by a series of damp sucking noises, closely followed by more hearty swearing.

By the time I reached her Alison was upright again but distinctly slimier than last time I saw her. To add to the drama, she stood in a position only normally possible after years of ballet training or a few sessions on a medieval torture device, with one leg knee deep in the bog.

'Hello precious', I ventured. 'You know, brown suits you...matches your eyes...'

I won't trouble you here with her response, but it cleared the hillside of sheep. A good heave-ho and a muddy hug later and we were on our way again.

Progress was slow but mostly downhill, resting on bracken covered bumps of safe ground before plunging on over the unforgiving terrain. Eventually we were within yards of the track but found our route tantalisingly out of reach across not one, but two streams of filthy gurgling viciousness. I leapt over the first and turned to help my mud encrusted beloved but instead found her striding through with a look that defied any act of God or nature to do its damnedest to stop her. It wasn't exactly the Red Sea, but nature knew when to concede and so with nothing more than mucky boots she hopped over the second ditch, up onto the trail, scattered a herd of Highland cows and strode off up the track.

I caught up and gently turned her around to face the correct way and by the time we reached the car we were chatting about the adventures we'd had on Mull, all the little things that we loved, our jobs, the scenery and from somewhere under a layer of mud and slime Alison said.

'You know what, we could always come back next year...'

* * *

Our jobs had become a lifestyle for us. We'd made new friends, enjoyed ever changing scenery, seen wildlife in abundance, delved into the rich history of the island and its inhabitants and, running through it all, we'd developed a deep and abiding love of Mull.

At times we missed family and friends, but with social media and the occasional trip south we kept in touch. We missed the convenience of popping over the road to the shop if we ran out of anything...then we learned to cope, to plan ahead and not rely on a choice of five supermarkets, three convenience stores, seven take-aways and six pubs within a 10-minute walk of our front door. Then we learnt to love having burns tumbling into the loch beside us, wooded hills, snow on the peaks, the sun setting through a gap in the mountains, seeing deer, sheep, lambs, otters, eagles and having friends and strangers alike offering to lend us a loaf of bread, a few litres of petrol or just pop by to see that we were okay and ask if we would 'like a cosy bed for the night when the storm hits rather than risk it in your motorhome?'.

* * *

Our last evening of the season on Mull was a wild night, the rain lashed down, the wind howled and shook everything. It helped that we were fortified by a few drinks with friends and a sobering walk back to Mavis in the wet and windy darkness.

The following morning, we left with mixed emotions... mostly sadness but a tingle of excitement for the journey ahead and a prickle of expectation at seeing family, friends and our house. On the ferry we held ourselves together until we passed work and friends and colleagues were out flying flags to send us on our way.

Tears flowed.

We waved goodbye to Mull through a rainbow and headed into the mist for a date with the Queen of the Moorlands.

EIGHTEEN

Joy Street

We had bought a house in Leek at the tail end of 2016, as we were coming to the end of our year on the road. As we said at the time 'the thing that most endeared Leek to us was the fact that it's an honest town, its people unpretentious and friendly.'

As everyone we knew said at the time. 'Where?'

Leek, known as The Queen of the Moorlands, sits on the edge of the Staffordshire Moorlands in the West Midlands, close to the Peak District National Park.

It was home, briefly, to William Morris, textile designer, revolutionary socialist, poet and key member of the 'arts and crafts' movement. While staying in Leek working on improving textile dyes, he became aware of the appalling conditions of the textile mills, which then helped cement his socialist political outlook.

Before Morris swaggered into town the area had already dallied with revolutionary politics. In 1842, Josiah Henry, a 19-year-old shoemaker from the town was shot through the head and killed by troops at nearby Burslem. Josiah had been among a horde of

Chartists, marching, and perhaps indulging in a little light rioting on the side, in protest at their poor working conditions and the corrupt political system of the day. Stoke and the potteries were among several poor industrial areas where the Chartist movement took root. Their demands were not unreasonable by today's standards:

- A vote for every man twenty-one years of age, of sound mind, and not undergoing punishment for a crime.
- A secret ballot to protect the elector in the exercise of his vote.
- Qualification to become a Member of Parliament should not be dependent on property ownership.
- Payment for Members of Parliament, thus enabling tradesmen, working men, or other persons of modest means to leave or interrupt their livelihood to attend to the interests of the nation.
- Equal constituencies, securing the same amount of representation for the same number of electors, instead of allowing less populous constituencies to have as much or more weight than larger ones.
- Annual Parliamentary elections, to prevent bribery, corruption and intimidation.

Poor Josiah was, at just 19 years old, already a widower with 3 young children when he was felled.

* * *

By the end of the 18th century Leek was a silk town and its silk mills employed around 2,000 people in the town itself and a further

1,000 in the wider neighbourhood. The mills were notoriously grim to work in.

Significant portions of the workforce were children, often from local workhouses. It is quite likely that Josiah's orphaned children ended up in one. High numbers of orphans meant local authorities were only too willing to place the children in the care of the mills to save them the expense of raising them. In the mill they would begin work aged around nine in return for food, lodgings and if they were lucky, one hour of schooling a week. The hours were long and the work unpleasant and often downright dangerous. The Macclesfield Courier printed this in May 1823, 'A little girl about seven years of age was caught by her clothes and drawn between an upright shaft in the engine room and a wall...life was extinct'. It's just one of many such entries in the local press of the time.

As if the hours weren't punishing and the conditions weren't hellish enough, the children were controlled by brutish stewards or 'overlookers'. On 23rd November 1833 The Macclesfield Courier reported on the death of 11-year-old Sarah Stubbs, who worked in a Macclesfield mill. The inquest revealed that she was repeatedly beaten for not tying broken silk threads at the required rate.

The work of children was sanctioned by law. The Cotton Factories Regulation Act of 1819 set the minimum working age at 9 and maximum working hours at 12, but later the Ten Hours Bill of 1847 limited working hours to 10 for children and women. Ironically in the early 1800's the silk mills were considered relatively benign places for children to work, to the extent that they were exempted from the child labour laws for a time. Looking back on it now the children working in the coal and lead mines were probably worse off but when we're talking about 10-year old's it's all relative.

A Parliamentary enquiry eventually uncovered and publicised some of the unsavoury conditions, which did lead to improvements.

Nevertheless, children were still employed. This is 10-year-old Samuel Downe, giving evidence to a parliamentary enquiry in 1832.

'We used to generally begin at five o 'clock in the morning till eight at night'.

When asked had he received punishment he replied. 'Yes, I was strapped most severely till I could not bear to sit upon a chair without pillows, and I was forced to lie upon my face at night. I was put upon a man's back and then strapped by the overlooker'.

When asked why he was punished he replied... 'I had never been in a mill where there was machinery, and it was winter time, and we worked by gaslight, and I could not catch the revolutions of the machinery to take the tow out of the hackles; it requires some practice and I was timid at it.'

The Education Act of 1880 introduced compulsory schooling up to the age of 10 and child labour began to decline. Subsequent amendments raised the school-leaving age to 12, with dispensations to leave before this age if pupils reached the required standards in reading, writing and arithmetic. By the end of Queen Victoria's reign, almost all children were in school up to the age of 12.

* * *

One thing the mill owners did do towards the turn of the century was to build housing for the workers and their families. Thus by 1878 the street in Leek where our house is was on the map.

The cobbled alleys are still there, as they are all over Leek, glorious in their evocation of a bygone age. But lest we sentimentalise too much, today we have mains drainage, indoor plumbing, central heating and refuse collection. We have an indoor toilet, a bathroom and a kitchen with gas at the flick of a switch rather than us having to fetch coal to feed the range.

I'm under no illusions about coal fires and range cooking. We had coal fires when my parents moved us to Suffolk. I was around 11 years old at the time. Bewitching as the crackling flames and flickering glow was, the fire needed careful nurturing all day and only heated a semicircle of our living room to a radius of about 3ft; anything inside the heating zone would steam and wither while anything outside froze. I spent many a winter evening on the threshold of the magical zone slowly revolving like a chicken on a rotisserie.

Every 15 minutes or so a plume of acrid smoke would puff back into the room where it joined the fug from my father's cigar to make my eyes sting and add another layer to the brown patina on the ceiling. On a bad night I'd bend double and cough up my dinner, my hair singed, and my bottom turned to ice. In between these smoky interludes I kept busy trying to avoid the red-hot embers the fire would spit out. These tiny incendiary bombs would burn on contact with flesh, burrow a smoky trail through clothes and occasionally ignite the dog. My school blazer looked like it belonged to a clumsy chain smoker lacking opposable thumbs. Garments dried on the old wooden clothes horse in front of the fire would crisp and stiffen up like board and had to be removed before they became dangerously flammable. I once made my freshly dried trousers stand up by themselves and then balanced a shirt on top to create a freestanding dummy fresh from the clothes horse.

Well, it was a long winter and there wasn't much else to do.

We had one radiator in the house, essentially an overflow for the coal fired back boiler in the range. It was in my bedroom and worked a treat, so long as you didn't mind desert conditions all summer and artic winters. If I turned it off in the summer the whole system would rumble ominously, and steam would escape from mysterious valves in the bathroom. If I turned it on in winter my room just got colder. The whole system was a mystery to my parents and, it turned out, to the local plumber too. I woke up one morning to a fountain of scalding water arcing across the room onto my bed. The plumber turned lots of valves and taps that had no noticeable effect, hit pipes with a hammer and generally walked about the place looking bemused. Eventually he repaired the radiator with some sort of putty and what looked suspiciously like a used bandage and I was advised to move my bed further away.

My mother used the coal fired range for cooking, which meant it cooked either with the power of a match under a cauldron or with the heat of a medium sized star. Added to this was her charming belief that the food would be ready when she was, despite the wildly fluctuating temperature of the oven and her aptitude for getting distracted. Remarkably dinner was always ready at 5.45pm.

If, that is, we accept the premise that 'ready' means it'll be served up in whatever state it happens to occupy at 5.45pm while on its haphazard journey from raw to carbonized.

So, all things considered Alison and I decided against open fires.

* * *

We began to integrate ourselves into the community; the people were very friendly once you got past the part of the introduction where they expressed surprise that we'd chosen to live in their town.

To help become familiar with the area one of the first things we did once we'd moved back in was go to the football.

We have always liked lower or non-league football, real football as we call it. Real not so much as in the action on the pitch, although that does have a more robust and direct approach to the game than the Premier League, but more on the stands and terraces. It's there from the moment you approach the ground; the fading sponsorship ads and peeling paintwork, the Day-Glo stewards who greet regulars and offer a polite nod to newcomers, the narrow turn-styles with their caged attendants armed with a stack of coins to make change, carefully ticking off each entrant type on their clipboard before their foot releases the turnstile for you to squeeze through, and the time-honoured banter in the queue, talk of 'our Darren' being selected for Thursday night training and swapping stories of the last match.

'9-0 away, bloody marvellous it was, like the old days...'

'Aye, but they'll need to be switched on today...can't get complacent...'

Inside, both sets of fans mingle, red and black scarves and discreet pin badges for the visiting team supporters, up for a cup match. They wandered around looking for a suitable place to stand without upsetting any locals, heaven forbid that you should accidentally stand where Old Bob always stands with his pie and lukewarm tea. Hardened home fans behind their goalkeeper, the same at the other end for the away supporters, friendly repartee, a few nods and polite hellos to the home fans as they pass. Rivals on the pitch maybe but recognising kindred spirits on the terraces, hardened by long drives and 0-0 draws on damp Tuesday nights. A hundred cups of instant coffee in a hundred different grounds, talk on the bus home of not bothering next season, but knowing that they will.

The coaching team shout and cajole from their dugouts, animated managers kick every ball and feel every collision while they bark orders from the touchline, holding their breath as a free kick is floated over, head in hands as a chance is missed, screaming into the wind and for 90 minutes, just a scarlet-faced bellow away from a coronary.

But the real experts are behind the painted fencing, with its pools of dried gloss and blooms of rust. These are the vocal supporters, squeezed into replica shirts and chomping on pie and chips while they berate everyone on the pitch for not being fit enough. Every move that breaks down, each mistimed challenge or error attracts a flurry of derision. Every interception attempt on goal or good save draws encouragement and praise. These are of course reversed when yelling at the visiting team when every move is roundly mocked.

It's nothing though compared to the abuse the referee gets. It truly is a thankless task because neither team nor their supporters are on the referee's side. They can do no right even when they are demonstrably correct in their decision. The torrent of invective some fans directed at the match officials was just plain nasty, lacking any of the wit and imagination that often springs from the terraces.

At half time we queued for refreshments. The menu offered 'pie', no fillings specified, with a variety of accompaniments chosen it seemed for their stomach lining properties; chips, gravy, peas (mushy of course), curry sauce, or hot dogs for the culinary daring; fodder for cold winter nights under the icy glare of floodlights.

The game itself was fun, passionate and occasionally enlivened by endearing incompetence; slips, headers going in the wrong direction, missed opportunities and occasionally outbreaks of the beautiful game.

Somehow Leek won 3-2, a fact that was hotly contested by the away fans who let the match officials know their feelings in no uncertain terms. There was a post-match scuffle in the players' tunnel, pulses quickened, testosterone sloshed about, before the teams were ushered off and the visiting supporters[xix] resumed their roll call of injustices to closed doors and grinning stewards.

We were rather buoyed up by the experience, even though we weren't certain which were the home team we were supporting until 10 minutes into the game.

As we left my attention was drawn to the sponsors; Povey's oatcakes, a vaping shop with an instantly forgettable name, a local electrical store and most prominent of all the ground and kit sponsors, Esterchem. The hoardings above both goal-end terraces helpfully listed some of their products to tempt you into the exciting adventures you could enjoy with Triacetin, Diacetin, Egda and other chemicals that I'm guessing aren't on every supporters shopping list.

On the other hand, without these sponsors who are unlikely to ever recoup what they spend, then teams like Leek Town wouldn't survive.

* * *

A young lad stood with his father, warming their hands around cups of hot Bovril, their breath steaming together in the chilly air. Precious moments spent discussing tactics, remembering past encounters and debating the referee's decisions. Maybe the father did this with his dad too, back when the home crowd was comfortably in four figures every Saturday. Side by side, their shadows split into four under the floodlights.

When it's all over they'll hunch up their shoulders, thrust hands deep into pockets and walk home together, darting across roads while analysing the game. It might be the only day of the week they spend with each other.

For a moment all is still and quiet except for the echo of old chants and cheers, the lingering smells of tobacco and beer, the stains of drinks spilt when the team scored, tears when the last game of the season confirmed relegation, or perhaps promotion; memories that haunt the ground as each generation adds another layer. Like the peeling barrier they are leaning upon, nostalgia and melancholy get tangled in a fleeting glimpse of a past etched into the soul of these crumbling grounds where the rituals get passed on from parent to child up and down the country.

With that sobering thought I'm off to grab some Esterchem 1,3 BGDA before the shops close.

NINETEEN

Radio Song

We were able to take advantage of our time in Leek to explore a bit. We walked to the nearby village of Rudyard, which boasts an impressive reservoir built to feed the local canal. This was where Rudyard Kipling's parents met, hence his unusual first name. I guess he was lucky that they didn't meet at nearby Tittesworth Reservoir.

It's all very nice as a touristy destination. There is a miniature railway that runs along one bank which I later found out had come from Mull, where it once ran visitors from the ferry terminal to Torosay Castle. At the reservoir there are myriad splashy pursuits involving boats and other buoyant contraptions and a circular walk of, and here I am quoting the official information board 'about 4 or 5 miles,' which seems curiously vague for such a short path. We can measure the distance to the moon and be out by fractions of a millimetre so being so imprecise about the length of a Sunday afternoon stroll is either charmingly endearing or bloody irresponsible. I'm drawn towards the latter.

Alison treated me to tea and a scone in a vain effort to stop me grumbling about the sign, following which we watched a squirrel eating an abandoned sandwich, which turned out to be remarkably entertaining.

We wandered back through Rudyard. The village is most comely, set on a wooded hillside overlooking the reservoir and Churnet valley. There is a smattering of newish bungalows and plenty of older cottages, all strung out along quiet streets. It's very tidy and quintessentially English, and smelled of sewage.

We passed a lad of maybe 14 or 15 herding reluctant Highland cows into a pen and thought of home...then realised that by home we meant Mull and not our house up the road.

* * *

We listened to songs that reminded us of Mull, ones we'd had on constant rotation in Mavis or in the car going to or from work. I also listened to a lot of radio over the winter while I was decorating, including a station local to Leek that delighted me in its clumsiness. Ludicrously cheerful presenters would interview guests who were barely monosyllabic, phone-ins would have callers who had no idea why they'd called up, or worse still, the 'usual suspects' like Stan from Biddulph who always had an opinion, be it on human rights; 'We didn't have 'em when I were young...' or feminine hygiene. 'I dunno what the fuss is about...' or cheese. 'Can't beat a bit of mouldy blue with a cracker...'.

My favourite piece was a daily quiz they ran where after practically pleading for people to phone in they started giving easier and easier clues until someone finally gave in and called, probably just to shut them up.

'We have Margery from Longsdon on the line...'

'Hello...Hello?'

'Hello Margery...you are live on Moorlands FM...I think you have an answer to our quiz?'

'Hello?'

'Hello Margery?

'Hello Nigel'

'It's Pete but never mind so Margery, earlier I asked the listeners of Moorlands FM "What popular singer was christened Harry Webb?" and your answer is?'

Well Nigel, is the answer Antony Eden? xx

Somewhere in this maelstrom of banality a piece about enforcing train by-laws caught my ear. Apparently 'bad language' on the local lines could now incur a fine and this got me wondering about how we see the world and our priorities.

For example, you can open your daily paper on the 07:15 into Kings Cross and read about famine, genocide, rape, torture, domestic violence, nuclear missile tests, all manner of political shenanigans and if, in response to such horrors, you mutter a horrified swearword you are liable to a penalty because you may upset someone. If you choose to be more offended by a four-letter word than you are about famine, genocide, rape, torture, domestic violence, nuclear missile tests and political shenanigans then I cannot help but think you may have your priorities wrong. Sure, it is easier to stop someone uttering a profanity than to end domestic violence, but I know which one offends me more.

And then fate played a winning hand.

On our way back from a trip to London we travelled First Class thanks to Virgin Rail only charging £2:00 extra per ticket. Just as we were working out which of the complimentary drinks would cost more than the £2 extra we'd paid a couple of complete tossers sat down immediately behind us. Well dressed, well-spoken tossers who were drunk to point of being loud and obnoxious but sadly not comatose, and even more sadly, not dead.

They made the whole carriage a miserable playground for their childish banter. A couple of women walking past were treated to howling and called dogs, when a guard asked them to refrain, they were almost polite until he was out of earshot when one declared. 'You don't get that in cattle class'.

On and on it went in a haze of alcohol laced swearing, homophobic and sexist mockery and general boorish boasting. While one went to the toilet the other watched hardcore porn on his phone at full volume.

We complained to the attendant and were given a bottle of wine as recompense. Sadly, the bottle was made of plastic and thus useless as a bludgeon.

We left them arguing loudly about an employee (Peter) who is 'on the make' and taking backhanders from contractors and who wasn't fired after his disciplinary hearing, a confidential conversation laced with profanities and conducted in a public space within earshot of the whole carriage.

So well played fate, I now feel contrite and understand that the occasional swear is fine if it's in a good cause so long as it's not accompanied by a prolonged bout of boorish, sexist drivel spouting from a spoilt, indiscrete fuckwit.

* * *

Apart from that incident our winter in Leek passed in comfort. We went to football, went to church, went on hikes and made friends. Alison went to work at a school in Stoke while I decorated the house, volunteered at the food bank and wrote a book. We visited old friends and made new ones, managed to see some bands and binge watched all the TV we'd missed over the summer.

We liked Leek, we liked the people, its charming pubs, cobbled streets, ancient market square and thriving arts scene. We liked our cosy little house where friends and family came to stay. We liked the scenery, the proximity of The Peak District National Park and the convenience of supermarkets, restaurants and take-aways.

But if truth be told our hearts were still on Mull, so when March was young, we said goodbye to family and friends, let the house, freed Mavis from her winter incarceration and headed north.

TWENTY

Take Us Back

When we got back to Mull we had a couple of days free to remind us of the joys and frustrations of living there. We explored Uisken, a remote cluster of houses set around a sandy cove with rocky islands to explore when the tide's out. We arrived in sunshine, admired the views over to the Isle of Jura, wandered across the sand, breathed in the salty air and at the furthest point from shelter, had a good nose around the largest of the islands; where we got caught in a hailstorm.

Bedraggled and gently steaming we headed back to the car, set off towards home and got caught behind a Ford Pootle – which is a generic term we've adopted for any car that drives along at the exact speed to prevent safe overtaking, too slow for comfort and that doesn't pull over in any of the amply provided passing spaces. Pootle drivers are the antithesis of Audi drivers. They are usually piloted by people who are completely oblivious of everyone and everything else around them. They seem to be interested only in swerving all over the road while scanning the countryside for anything they can't see in their native suburbia, like cows, sheep or the inside of a loch as they plunge in after spotting a crow.

There is of course far more interesting wildlife on Mull than crows. To spot the most elusive, to us anyway, of Mull's rare breeds we tried otter spotting from a hide. Spoiler alert - we didn't see any. What we did encounter was Gerald and Margery, ancient bird spotters.

It had all started well; we were ensconced in our little hide with another couple, who took their leave after successfully identifying the Spanish frigate F101 as she sailed down the Sound of Mull. After a few moments of precious silence during which otters were probably mustering in their hundreds ready to entertain us with a display of synchronised frolicking, the door flew open and in rustled Gerald and Margery, or rather Gerald and a tripod with some sort of scope under his arm. Margery eventually wrestled her tripod through the door which she then closed with a clunk that echoed off the mountains.

I suspect that they arrived in a Ford Pootle or its close relative the Vauxhall Dawdle.

After exchanging a knowing look with Alison that involved much theatrical raising of eyebrows and rolling of eyes we settled back to our vigil. Gerald now started assembling his tripod while his waterproof outfit squeaked out an accompaniment to his every move. As if this wasn't nerve jangling enough, he breathed extravagantly through his mouth the whole time with a phlegmy rattle. Just as he completed assembling his super-duper-extreme-deluxe-view-o-scope on its tripod Margery opened the window in front of her in a series of creaks, bangs and scrapes which sent birds into the air.

'See the... (gasp for breath) ...Great Northern Diver...(wheeze)...over here... (gasp...splutter)... Margery...(rustle rustle, cough)... at about 11:00 O'clock ... (gasp, pant)...from the third buoy...(wheeze)...on the (rattle, squeak) ... left...(gasp)...eh?'

Margery seemed less than impressed and grunted a non-committal 'umm' that managed to communicate in one single syllable a whole lifetime of frustration living with Mr Wheezy Excitement. Of course, that's pure conjecture, I suspect they are adorable people and very much in love, but I was a trifle exasperated at not seeing anything more exciting than oyster catchers from our snug hideaway.

The oyster catcher is the one bird I have a soft spot for. This comical black and white creature with its long orange beak has us both entranced. Oyster catcher may sound like it stalks its quarry across the ocean floor in a stealthy battle between hunter and prey, but oysters aren't known for doing much at all and are certainly not fleet of foot; basically, they're just a stone with a soft centre. Catching one requires little more than dipping into the water at a likely spot.

They are endearingly comical to watch though. They waddle along with a clumsy gait, chirp away with their over-long orange bills and occasionally stab at the kelp on the shoreline, although I have never witnessed one catch anything. We've watched them for ages and probably missed white tailed eagles carry deer off to their nests as we did. I'm not sure if oyster catchers join the dawn chorus, but if they do, they'll be the ones put into the back row and told not to let everyone else down by fidgeting, picking their nose or pretending to be an aeroplane.

The dawn chorus starts nice and early around here and may be part of the reason I was feeling a little irritable with Gerald and Margery. It can begin as early as 4.30am when a goose will let forth a solo honk. Even the most dedicated ornithologist cannot really call the sound of a goose attractive. At best it sounds like a clown blowing his nose, at worst, at 4:30am for example, like a clown blowing his nose on a handkerchief stained with the blood of his latest victim.

Other birds soon join in with more delicate but no more welcome calls. After 10 minutes or so I usually add a quilt rippling fart to the cacophony, turn over and fall asleep, or maybe pass out, but either way 20 seconds later I am jolted awake by that bloody goose again.

I like birds in the same way I like sunshine and flowers. They are very pleasant, and the world would be worse off without them but except for watching oyster catchers make fools of themselves I don't feel the need to study them or take more than a passing interest. I leave that to the serious looking folk like Gerald and Margery with their tidy notebooks and matching waterproof clothes.

* * *

My first customer of season two was a Canadian visitor who tried to pay for entry with an old paper £10 note. I pointed out that we could no longer accept it and he apologised and tipped out a purse full of coins saved from previous visits to the UK. Among the horde scattered over the counter were two sixpence pieces.

Now I know dear reader that you are young and tender in years so for those of you who don't recall the sixpence, this tiny silver nugget somehow escaped decimalisation in 1971 and eventually went out of circulation in 1980 when it was worth $2\frac{1}{2}$ new pence.

My father was a company accountant at the time of decimalisation. Although I was too young to really appreciate the stress this caused him, I do recall being instructed on the new currency and his exasperation at having to manually change every record in a world before computerisation.

He had volumes of books filled with conversion tables, while my mother armed herself with a plastic decimal converter, a hand-held plastic gizmo with 2 or 3 little windows and wheels to spin, the idea being to display the decimal amount in one window, and it would display the imperial equivalent in the other– or visa-versa. I seem to recall it was about the size of her handbag, bright red and never worked properly.

By 1971 nearly the entire world used a decimal system based on units of 10 – making arithmetic easy to perform in our heads or on fingers (and toes if necessary). The old imperial system it was replacing in Britain was a legacy of Roman times; there were 20 shillings to the pound and 12 pennies to the shilling. Therefore, there were 240 pennies to a pound, making my Canadian chums sixpence originally worth one-fortieth of a pound.

Until the 60's there were farthings to contend with too. A farthing was worth ¼ of a penny. According to people who cherish nostalgia over reality, armed with a single farthing you could purchase your weekly shop, have a slap-up meal and still have enough change to buy a house on your way home. I once found two farthings on my way to primary school and thought that I was now rich beyond my wildest dreams. I bought some pink shrimp sweets and a comic with them.

With the demise of imperial money went the Empire, cricket on the village green, unbroken sunshine from May to October and saluting the Union Flag. Well, maybe I exaggerate slightly but predictably decimalisation gave the self-righteous publicity seekers plenty of opportunity to become 'metric martyrs.' Local TV was full of ruddy faced butchers and angry greengrocers expressing faux concern for the poor pensioners...because clearly a generation that won a world war or two, created the NHS, the computer, umpteen domestic and medical advances and went into space couldn't be trusted to grasp counting on their fingers.

But never mind all that, our Commonwealth friend rounded up enough legal tender to gain admission and I settled back into my familiar perch in the kiosk, waited for my next customer and enjoyed the view.

The weather…well improved would be an accurate description. When we arrived back on Mull a grey mist draped itself over the landscape, sucking out the colour and flattening the view until everything was just shadows, echoes of the mountains and trees that we knew so well.

Now the colours were coming back, vivid green fields with ribbons of brown that traced tumbling stone walls and shimmering trees of radiant green poking out from their muted brown neighbours. Whole hillsides sprung to life, seemingly overnight, with fresh grass competing with the unfurling bracken for the watery sunlight. The scent of wild garlic mixed in with the sweet woody aroma of gorse and the tang of the sea. It's at moments like this that our lifestyle makes perfect sense.

From my kiosk I heard tyres crunching over the car park and turned to watch a tidy little car meticulously reverse into the exact centre of a parking space, pull forward, repeat the manoeuvre until it is rested in precisely the same spot as it was on its first attempt.

After a couple of minutes, the doors opened, slowly. There was a faint rustling on the breeze, a familiar wheezing and Gerald and Margery slowly unfurled from their Pootle.

It was a long afternoon.

TWENTY-ONE

Complications

The Ford Pootle may be fictitious but I've never really been one for car culture so I couldn't tell you what Gerald and Margery really arrived in. I have never coveted getting behind the wheel of anything appointed with more luxury than a functioning heater and radio but I had reason soon after Gerald and Margery's visit to borrow a lavishly appointed car to ferry Alison back from dropping off our Mazda for its MOT.

It was a scary experience.

Firstly, I had to start the damn thing. What I had mistaken for a handy receptacle for loose change turned out to be a port for the key fob which, once deposited, allowed the car to start...

Or rather didn't...at least not until I'd accidentally pressed the correct sequence of buttons when, to my alarm the interior lit up like a Christmas tree, beeped, flashed and whirred in a fashion that would have delighted a toddler or a 17-year-old called Wayne but terrified the bejesus out of me. Even the arm rest had more buttons than our car needs to function successfully. Finally, it settled into an impatient humming sulk while I worked out that the handbrake was a switch buried somewhere out of sight below the steering wheel and required nothing more of me than a gentle prod to release 2 litres of finest Swedish engineering backwards at 70 miles an hour.

Until that hair-raising moment my attention had been focused entirely on trying to figure out which of the many gears would result in forward momentum. I tried all of them at least twice before we finally lurched ahead in a series of crunching hops.

I realise now that it is quite a good idea to acquaint oneself with the basic controls before setting off. Had I done so I would have known where reverse was, that it had six gears, not four as I'd thought for the first few miles of our journey, and I wouldn't have had to stop twice within ½ a mile of leaving home. Once to find out where the windscreen wiper control was (in the boot possibly, I never did find out) and once to try and turn the heating down from thermo nuclear to tropical paradise.

Once underway again I made reasonable progress, even successfully indicating right by pounding every stalk on the steering column. I had wanted to turn left but after seeing the look on the face of the driver in the car following, I decided to stick to the direction the car had chosen, to his evident relief as he vanished in a cloud of dust.

Around 10 minutes into the journey I discovered the word 'cruise' etched into the steering wheel. Maybe it came equipped with its own guided missile system I thought, those canny Swedes pretending to be neutral and all the time arming their family saloons with the means to launch a pre-emptive strike on Norway and steal their fjords. While absentmindedly musing upon Scandinavian conflict I became aware of a slowly increasing warmth in the rump. I felt between my legs and the seat was reassuringly dry but alarmingly hot. I guessed what I earlier thought was the control for the radio had in fact been the seat warmer so I took the only sensible course of action and twisted, punched, pummelled and mashed every button, knob and switch within reach until the hairs on my posterior were no longer sizzling away in their own juices.

I had no idea how the climate control system worked. Every so often a puff of warm damp air would escape from a vent in the dashboard and warm the empty passenger seat or a cold draft would suddenly chill my left ankle until it got bored. I tried a likely looking knob with a red crescent fading into a blue one, but this only succeeded in turning the radio on. So now accompanied by Radio 4 with sporadic interruptions on the traffic situation in Gdansk I settled in for all of two minutes.

I could see the roadworks in good time, and thanks to their luminous coats also the two men with their STOP/GO boards standing at each end of a digger that was clearing goodness knows what from a ditch, possibly all the decaying otters that Adrian Derry had left after his visit. There was no traffic following me and nothing approaching from the other direction, so, seeing me approach one of them decided to switch from GO to STOP, presumably because they'd had nothing else to do all morning. I jerked down through a few random gears to a dead stop, whereupon he switched immediately to GO.

Of course he did...I was just thinking about how he might not be sufficiently qualified to do a job where the sole requirement is the ability to hold a stick, when I stalled the car and had to go through the whole pre-flight routine before crawling past him and his smirking colleague, then mistaking 2nd gear for 4th and screeching off in a cloud of rubbery smoke. I tried stabbing the 'cruise' button a few times but sadly no one in a high vis jacket exploded.

* * *

Roadworkers can be an easy target so out of interest I looked up the statistics and now have a renewed respect for the UK's 4000 or so high vis souls who are generally trying to earn a few bob while making our roads safer.

In 2016, 347 incidents of road worker abuse were reported, but fewer than half of the 23 companies who belong to the Highways Term Maintenance Association were asked to supply figures, so the real number is much higher.

Of those incidents, 267 were in the form of swearing, shouting, hand gestures and threats but the rest encompassed a smorgasbord of serious assaults that included; shooting, throwing of items such as screwdrivers, kicking, punching and beating, in one case with baseball bats. Not only that but accidental injuries and fatalities also happen because drivers frequently encroach into coned off areas (over 150 times a month according to Highways England), all because we want to get home in time to see which washed up non-entity has been expelled from the jungle this week.

A study by Oxford University in 2016 placed roadworkers as the 16th most dangerous occupation in the UK. Considering that some of the professions rated more dangerous have tiny work forces, like deep sea divers and bomb disposal experts, then manning the country's STOP/GO boards can be a perilous profession.

I didn't know any of that on my way home. By then I'd mastered most of the rudimentary controls, so I was able to glide to a gentle halt at the first STOP sign for exactly the length of time it took to turn a stick through 180 degrees.

Next time I'll be sure to give them a cheery wave and smile of acknowledgment as I drive past. Or at least a smile, I'm not sure lifting a hand from the combined steering wheel/gearstick/heater-control/guided-missile-system would be wise under the circumstances.

When I eventually arrived home, there were whole clusters of switches that I hadn't tried and lots of enticingly illuminated knobs remained untwiddled. Goodness knows what any of them do, I'm at a loss to account for anything short of a coffee maker that was missing from my journey.

* * *

We were lucky enough that the weather was unseasonably warm and dry. Without a car there were a whole host of chores to enjoy; cleaning, laundry, writing, all manner of little jobs that we ignored in favour of going for a local walk.

The summit of Carn Ban is only 249 metres, so we left the ropes and crampons at home, but the terrain and lack of any footpath for most of the way up made up for the absence of height and the sense of remoteness was palpable. The only people we met while out were on the road to the start of the walk. As soon as we got a couple of metres above sea level the only company we encountered were herds of skittish deer, buzzards and the call of cuckoos carried on the wind from the woodlands below.

The first leg was up and around Loch a'Ghleannain. Because of its exposed layers of ancient rocks geologists get very excited about Loch a'Ghleannain, but we don't, so we simply skirted its western flank and steadily rose higher and higher over its undulating slopes until we could look down to its wooded eastern bank and wonder at the views over Duart Castle and all the way to Ben Nevis over 40 miles away. We also wondered what sort of ill prepared dolts would attempt such an adventure on a hot day without sunscreen. Us, we concluded! Fortunately, the breeze encouraged us to keep an extra layer on to protect our arms from the unseasonal sunshine. The dry spell and sunshine also meant that the route we were on was only modestly challenging. When it rains a lot of this land becomes a gloopy quagmire and the rest undulating tussocks of greenery sticking up from deep peaty crevices. It looks splendid from a distance but up close it's the most unforgiving, frustrating, ankle snapping vicious landscape imaginable unless, like the day we chose to walk up, you can wade through dried up bogs and skip daintily along deer paths.

After a while we levelled out at an area where the route narrowed to a grassy ridge between steep cliffs, falling away to a plain at the south end of the loch or a sharp descent through ancient woodlands to the road to Grasspoint. We made for a small gate in the high deer fence and wondered that in such a remote spot there is evidence of human activity. The fence was fairly new, a year or two old probably, but for some of its course it followed a moss covered stone wall that could have been there for a century or more and at the narrowest point where we paused in a bluebell glade to admire the view an old iron post marked a fence line from sometime between the two eras.

From here on we were most definitely off-piste. We had to choose between climbing up or skirting around a bouldered escarpment ahead of us. After some consideration, not entirely unrelated to us getting our breath back, we opted for the short, sharp climb and set off hand over hand to a grassy plateau that fell slowly away to bring us back down but further along the ridge, then across a mostly dried up bog to a steep switchback climb up a ridge where a lone lichen covered tree clung on half way up, drawing whatever sustenance it could from its lonely hillside perch.

Again and again our walk up led us up then gently down but there was no realistic option but to press on and take each ridge in our ever shortening stride. After an encounter with the skeleton of a deer in a dry peat marsh, we found a handy rock and paused for lunch. We were on a plateau that fell gently away to the loch far below. In light diffused through hazy clouds the panorama below us was like a Victorian painting of the highlands, a mythical, romanticised version of land that in reality has constantly fought back against man-made intrusions; land where every plough was blunted and peat for fires had to be hewn from remote wind and rain swept marshes. Sheep and cows were grazed on these lands, high up where dour men with leathery faces built the walls and knew every inch of the land, the springs for clean water, the bogs to avoid, the fields for peat and the woods for shade, unlike us, who just flopped in the sun and silently chewed our sandwiches, exhausted and transfixed by the scenery.

I do love a nice plateau, the feeling of being up high on level ground where few have ventured. The effort of reaching it and its seclusion turned it into our own little piece of the world. Like a secret tree house as a child where you felt you could escape the clutches of the adult world for a while and be yourself. At least that was my experience of a treehouse, but as it was in the family garden, in full view of the house and about as high up as my father's head the secret was perhaps more in my imagination than reality. It was variously a base for launching commando raids on Nazis, a space station on the moon, the bridge of an aircraft carrier or battleship, the flight deck of a fighter plane or of my own personal Short-Sunderland Flying Boat (my all-time favourite aeroplane). Later it became a repository for illicit beer, much traded copies of Playboy, Mayfair and Hustler, cigarettes and for a short summer one end of the aerial for our own pirate radio station.

The station was a natural collaboration between my best friend of the time, a public school educated electronics nut who discovered the plans for building a small transmitter, and me, a comprehensive oik with a passion for music and pirate radio but who once tried to wire his record player directly into the mains to increase its volume. (Top tip, it doesn't work).

We broadcast on FM to a radius of about 2 feet. It was quieter listening on the radio than if we'd simply played the records on the HiFi. My friend moved onto legitimate amateur radio after frying every circuit in his parents' house while trying to boost our radius as far as the youth club. When he recovered the biscuit tin crammed with our (his) primitive circuitry from its hiding place in some bushes by the riverbank I found it had my name and address on the base in my mother's handwriting. I crossed off Supervillain from my career options. That just left Astronaut, Rock Star and Captain of the England Football Team. Walking to school the following day I wondered which one Mr Sullivan, the school careers advisor, would direct me towards? I wasn't in the school football team, couldn't sing or play an instrument and so I assumed I'd be in space in a year or two.

Instead I was sent, along with the rest of the class, to the careers office in town where we were taught how to sign on for unemployment benefit. I knew the Apollo missions were infrequent, but I had no idea we had to pay our own way between missions. This was an appalling way to treat a future hero and I made a mental note not to permit Mr Sullivan onto my spaceship when the Martians invaded, and we had to flee earth to colonise new worlds.

Back on our lonely plateau we packed up our lunch debris and followed more deer tracks until we took a steep track downhill to meet the Glennan Uachdarach path from Grasspoint, the route taken by the pilgrims en-route to the island of Iona. Livestock were sent in the other direction to cross from Grasspoint to the island of Kerrera, which was then just a short hop to the mainland and Oban.

It was only a short stretch on the track before it ran parallel to a stone wall, our cue to strike out upwards off the track and over rough ground until we eventually rounded a knoll and could see the trig point ahead on top of its isolated peak. We crossed a peat bed and slowly made our way up to the summit. It was breezy but the views were stunning in every direction, from the island of Jura across the Firth of Lorn to the peaks of Mull; Ben Buie, Ben More, Corrabheinn, Ben Taladh, Dun Da Gaoithe and its smaller sister Squrr Dearg. We paused for refreshment, talked about nothing and everything, about the views, which peak was which, what islands we were looking at, the rise of the far right in British politics, work, wildlife and why we forgot the sun cream. The only conclusion we came to was that forgetting the sun cream was foolish.

We walked to the edge of the peak to gaze down on the abandoned settlement of Galachaolish below us then set off retracing our steps down to the stone wall, picking up the track to a point where it met the old road to Galachaolish, now a footpath criss-crossed by deer paths and the tell-tale tracks of shepherd's 4x4 Quad bikes. It was a trudge back home in the heat, the climb and terrain had sapped our energy, our limbs ached and the final stretch was on the road with the bonus of coinciding with the arrival of a ferry at Craignure, so we were constantly leaping onto the verge to let cars, buses, motorhomes and lorries pass. Despite this rather soul sapping finale it was a terrific walk, challenging at times but it reminded us why we are here; wildlife, scenery, solitude and history. History that I looked up when we got back, starting with trying to find out what Carn Ban meant.

According to an on-line translation I tried it means 'pile of women'. Walking over it at no time were we reminded of a pile of women. In his book Walking the Mull Hills, Hamish Brown translates Carn Ban as pale or whitish hill, which seems more likely.

I like words like whitish, it saves all that nonsense with invented shades that are so beloved of paint manufacturers. If place names on Mull were allocated by Dulux Carn Ban would be called something like Translucent Ivory Peak.

I'd recently had cause to purchase some yellow paint. I described it as mustardy yellow.

'Do you mean Yellow Ochre?' said young Wayne, who looked like he was doing work experience but was wearing a duty manager badge, possibly by mistake.

'Aren't they black and white whales?'

There followed a pause while both of us did some mental shuffling. Wayne gave in first.

'It's darkish yellow, a kind of mustard colour, would you like to look at a paint chart?'

I looked. 'Oh, ochre, I though you meant...never mind... yes that'll be fine thank you.'

At least ochre is a natural pigment that is, surprise surprise, mustardy yellow so I suppose I shouldn't complain. But some of the colours they dream up don't bear resemblance to any spectrum I'm familiar with. Take these examples from Farrow & Ball: Savage Ground, Mole's Breath, and Peignoir. A Peignoir is a light dressing gown or negligee, so I'm imaging whatever colour it starts out as, it turns watery grey and has the texture of much laundered tissue paper. Presumably Mole's Breath is the colour of half-digested worm and Savage Ground could be anywhere in the range between flaming lava and arctic ice sheet but is actually a dull pink.

I don't want to single out Farrow & Ball, so I looked up Dulux and struggled to get beyond 'Old-school goes modern' on their website. Anyone who dreams up such meaningless nonsense probably has an equally pretentious palette I thought, and lo I wasn't wrong: Knight's Armour, Lucky Penny and, oh dear, Tunnel Vison.

'Darling, I was just wondering if we should spruce the place up, maybe a lick of paint and whatnot. I know, what's your favourite sensory ailment for the feature wall, I can't decide between Burst Eardrum or Tunnel Vision?

'Oh sweetie, they're both sooo 2018. What about something trendy like Fluffy Buffalo Anus or Bonsai Cardiac Popsicle?'

On I trawled. Crown Paints seemed to think I wanted an online immersive experience rather than to buy a tin of magnolia emulsion. I couldn't find a chart or list of their colours, but I do now know that monochrome is timeless, and that pink is 'in', so it wasn't a wasted encounter.

It was all rather soul destroying really and made us thankful that we could sit in Mavis and stare out at a landscape that comes in proper colours like red, yellow, green and blue. Exhausted from the trials of car technology and walking up hills, that evening we dived into a pile of DVDs we had bought at the local charity shop and selected a Hollywood superhero flick, put the kettle on, snuggled down and let ourselves be transported to a world of big budgets, stretchy costumes and plots with more holes than an international convention of sieve manufactures.

TWENTY-TWO

Heroes

Robert loved Superheroes. He even had a Captain America themed hallway in his flat, the flat he'd lived in for a few years and was his pride and joy. His place to flop, leave untidy if he wished, stack dirty washing up beside the sink, leave the vacuum cleaner alone for a while, put the TV on, grab a coffee and do sod all. Or dive into the washing up, polish every surface, balance the TV remote on the mantlepiece and plump every cushion to marshmallow fluffiness. This was his domain, to do with as he pleased, his Avengers Tower. (I entered a whole cyber universe populated by intelligent, well-adjusted adults when I looked up where Captain America lived.[xxi])

He had wanted his own place for as long as I remember. An aspiration that most if not all of us share. Somewhere to be ourselves. To control and keep as we feel fit, away from parental rules, the judgement of our peers and where we can, for example, create a Superhero themed hallway if we want to.

And why not.

Many people thought that having a place to call his own was a dream too far for Robert. After all, when you start towards the back of the field, and the rules are regularly changed according to fashion and political whim, the race is going to be stacked against you from day one. Being born with a learning disability, in Roberts's case Down Syndrome, means your chances, your aspirations, hopes and dreams are going to face extra challenges and that illusive home of your own will more than likely remain a dream.

Robert, like thousands of others in a similar situation, faced a lifetime of odd looks, sneers, open hostility, patronising, prejudice and social isolation. He was fortunate to have a close family who worked tirelessly to help him achieve his independence and get his precious flat.

He may have loved superheroes, but what Robert aspired to, and reached, was a regular domestic life as modelled not by preening crimefighters wearing too much Lyrica but by regular joes. People who choose their own shower gel, struggle back from the supermarket with groceries, hang their laundry out, choose to decorate their hallway as they wish, and get to shut their own front door and lock it with their own key. Simple achievements that we take for granted but for some they mean the difference between a life spent dreaming of what could be or one spent living that dream.

That didn't stop the occasional idiot making stupid remarks in his presence and undermining his confidence. It amazes me that people think that their words just bounce off without doing harm.

But they do harm...the choices we make in our language, the words we choose, the people we ignore or engage with, it all matters.

* * *

A red faced and sweaty bloke cycled up to the kiosk while Alison was in it. He arrived ahead of his two mates and asked Alison if we did a discount for someone who is retarded?

Not knowing the circumstances, she replied that we did a discount for people who have a disability, including a learning disability. He smiled and said it was for his mate who's 'a bit retarded.'

He wasn't, except maybe being held back socially by his friend's lack of cultural sensitivity. Retarded, in the context of an intellectual disability is such an ugly word to our ears. It wasn't always so and in some parts of the world it is still in common use and perhaps hasn't attracted the negative connotations that it's acquired here.

Some words attract stigma as they age, like once fresh milk they turn sour and rancid. What was once acceptable becomes taboo. Words like idiot, moron and spastic were all acceptable medical terms that passed into slang. Not because they were affectionate cuddly words, but because they were used as weapons to bully people by comparing them to persons deemed less worthy and open to ridicule.

I once had a protracted argument with someone over their use of the word mong on an otherwise perfectly good website aimed at young people fighting depression ('don't just sit at home and mong out...') The crux of his argument was people don't care about the etymology of words. It wasn't until Robert's sister got involved and pointed out how the word mong was used to bully both her and her brother that he relented, albeit with rather bad grace.

I don't claim any moral high ground here. As teenagers my friends and I would think nothing of referring to our local Chinese restaurant as the 'Chinky'. We meant no offence, but the children of the owners were bullied, de-personalised and set apart by our clumsy language. Some used the word queer in a derogatory sense too, intending to slander each other with accusations of homosexuality. How awful that sounds today - to suggest that being gay should be the subject of bullying is indefensible to me now.

One way that some people have sought to fight prejudice is by reclaiming words meant as pejorative, as the gay community has done with queer. They haven't eliminated homophobia or prejudice but the power of the word to wound is diminished and there is a sense that the push for equality, not just in law but in thought and deed, is in the right direction.

The same couldn't be said with any confidence about people who have learning disabilities. Self-advocacy seldom reaches far enough and is woefully underfunded, portrayal on TV and the press all too often concentrates on the whimsical and photogenic and not on the everyday struggles of rejection, fear, abuse and exclusion from the mainstream that the 1.5 million people in the UK who have a learning disability face. According to research by Mencap in the UK 82% of children with a learning disability are bullied[xxii].

Our language can be wonderfully colourful, it can express a whole range of experiences in a short sentence and be both complex and simple at the same time; for example, my thesaurus just suggested 29 synonyms for the word simple. Language can be subtle and build us up with compliments and attention or erode us over time with insults and slurs, and it can punch with words designed to wound.

Words have power but most of us can, at a pinch, reclaim them, redefine them if we choose to. We can reject what we once accepted as normal; I found a paint chart from the 1950's that included the colour 'nigger brown'. Only the most obtuse or die hard racist would consider that acceptable now.

You could make the argument that we choose to take offence, especially when we do so on behalf of others; maybe if no offence is intended then none should be taken?

Undoubtably, there are occasions when people can be over-sensitive and could be more resilient in a world that will not offer them safe spaces beyond their circle of associates.

But wherever you stand, the Roberts of this world, people with learning disabilities, are not choosing to take offence. The casual use of ugly words like retard and mong, even as a 'jokey' reference to each other, reinforces the stigma associated with being different. We can start to welcome people in from the margins and build a better, more inclusive society, person by person, community by community if we'd only stop and think about the power of a simple word.

All human life is of equal value. We are capable of great and unconditional love, we can create breath-taking works of art, compose music that reduces us to tears or euphoria, create medicines that cure diseases on a pan-global scale, give people new limbs and organs, put people on the moon, write books that change destinies, invent the internet, harness the sun, sea and wind. Heck, we can even split the atom and tickle a quark if we choose to. We've survived ice ages, epidemics, wars, famines and Bernard Matthews' Turkey Twizzlers. Not bad for a bunch of walking, talking bags of soggy meat, some of whom happen to be wired differently from those around them.

The irony here is that Robert was the person least likely to cause offence, judge others or condemn anyone. He accepted people for who they were. A simple enough skill you'd think but one that for all our good intentions most of us just can't seem to master.

* * *

Robert achieved his dream, thanks to his family, friends, campaigners, activists and pioneers who fought against institutions and prejudice, but mostly thanks to his own vision and determination.

Then one bright day in May, groggy from being woken by a buzzing phone I listened in shock while my tearful son told me that Robert had passed away in the night.

The world paused.

Alison and I hugged, bewildered and numb.

There were no words.

A shadow lay over our lives, and we were only on the periphery of Robert's life. His family were going through hell. We felt guilty every time we laughed or thought about trivial things like what we would have for dinner.

While people mourned and grappled with his passing, we carried on as normal, but other shadows were gathering.

Not that we knew that yet.

TWENTY-THREE

Didn't It Rain

We kept in touch with people around Robert, but felt that all we could realistically do was to offer support from a distance. Something about our mood was echoed in the weather as it switched from sunshine to rain, which in some ways suited our disposition but it didn't encourage us to get out much. On the advice of a friend we tried exploring old logging roads that afforded reasonably dry passage through cleared areas which would otherwise be inaccessible.

On one such track we found our way up to a waterfall in the clough of Dun da Ghaoithe, the second highest peak on Mull.

The air was damp, with mist rolling over the summit above us and settling like fine morning dew. The grasses were lush, deep greens alive with the scent of dank earth and decaying vegetation. Small pink flowers stood on spindly stalks near the side of the track, their heads soaking up the moist air and yellow flowers hugged the rocks between mosses and grassy peat, tangled with roots and insects.

It was the sort of area where my holidaying mother would have stooped down, plucked an attractive and probably rare and protected 'specimen' of local flora, carefully place it in a bag with a moistened tissue and once back at whatever shack my father had rented for us, lovingly position it with the others she'd collected during the week. Once back home they would be tenderly transplanted into our garden, for the dog to piss on or to be crushed by my football. Fortunately for both me and the dog she never knew because once planted she would forget all about them. Occasionally some particularly hardy specimen would survive everything the canine and schoolboy world could throw at it and burst into colourful life in the spring...when my father would immediately identify it as a weed and sling it onto the compost heap.

Today on our walk where the constant gurgling of the river was all consuming in this natural amphitheatre with its walls of mist, we clambered up to the fence line, erected not just to keep out deer and sheep but also to prevent human access to the small hydro-electric plant that feeds the properties below. The view down past the trees to the Sound of Mull and Morven on the opposite bank was lit up in watery sunlight while up here the hydro plant seemed incongruous, a man-made intrusion into the wilderness, although most of the 'wilderness' was managed forest land below us and sheep pasture above.

* * *

The track we took was one of several leading up into the hills, and the only one we'd followed that didn't end in the middle of nowhere. Most of them were built for the lorries that took the timber away, so they come to an abrupt halt in marshy clearings or in open patches that have previously been cleared and where self-seeded pines and gorse bushes are now reclaiming the land. The ground is recovering but even straying a few metres from the track you set foot in bogs or find impassable thickets. On a similar adventure we saw wonderful waterfalls cascading down hills, through gullies centuries in the making but tantalisingly out of reach to anyone not prepared for snorkelling through swamps or equipped with sturdy waders and a sharp machete.

Not that we are complaining, the area is unspoilt for a reason, improving access would ruin it and so we are content to admire it from a distance and marvel at the scale of these hills and mountains and enjoy what we can access in relative comfort.

For example, just south of Tobermory, the island's de-facto capital, Loch Aros is stunning. Even so close to what passes for civilisation here, on a hot day we had it almost to ourselves. Following a logging track that switch-backed down between tall pines we entered a high sided valley where the track petered out to a well-defined path. The trees drew in like sentries, their canopy providing us with welcome shade. Fresh pine and earthy mulch perfumed the air, insects buzzed, and long fingers of pale sunlight reached into the gloom, one of which pointed to the ruins of a small house improbably positioned amid tall trees.

Once it would have stood in a shallow glade with a small burn trickling through, perhaps with a vegetable plot that was someone's pride and joy, the fire grate blackened and a stack of peat drying beside it. Maybe a goat tethered in the yard with chickens pecking around its feet. Now it is a few crumbling walls at the end of a path beaten by the curious, ducking under fallen trees and stepping over broken tiles to explore the ruins.

What tales could this cottage tell of a time before the trees took over? Where did the people go? Were they happy here? Were they forced to leave? Did it become the last home for an old lady who waved her children off to new lives overseas where there was work and opportunity? Did she sit alone with her knitting for company as the encroaching trees cast longer shadows every year?

Probably not, but it was the kind of romantically bleak place that brought such images to mind. At least it wasn't made of gingerbread with an unfeasibly large oven or lined with the skulls of curious tourists.

We walked on, around the loch where we stood in sunlight and watched a shower sweep across the water without troubling us with anything but a few warm drops. Leaves on the trees shone in the diluted light, colours glowed, translucent greens and soft browns, pale blue water and pastel rocks glossy with fresh rain and warmed by dappled sunlight. We strolled around the loch on dirt and stone trodden down to a solid path but met only a couple of walkers and saw no one else apart from a father doing his best to entice a toddler to keep walking.

Climbing some steps up a side trail we watched white water cascade over the cliff in a tumbling waterfall. There is something transfixing about a waterfall; strong and powerful eating away the rock, yet scoop up a handful of water and it trickles away to nothing.

We walked back to the car.

Nothing dramatic happened, except that we realised that this place, this island, was in our souls and no amount of stress or strain could diminish its hold over us.

TWENTY-FOUR

All of The People

I'd found that sitting in a little kiosk selling tickets through a window, which is about 50% of my job, meant that I got to meet all sorts of people, for as long as it takes to conduct a simple transaction. Mostly, and I mean no disrespect by this, they are just anonymous faces at the window. Occasionally though characters or features grab my attention.

* * *

Wearing a formal white shirt with a tie from one of the older Oxford colleges, cream trousers and brown brogues that probably cost more than our house, he bumbled up the drive in a flurry of gesticulation. What should have been a 2-minute walk turned into 20 as he waylaid passers-by with improbable anecdotes, accompanied by so much waving of arms he may have been keeping up a simultaneous translation by semaphore. He carried an ageing thermos in his right hand that was wielded around like a club when he added emphasis. By the time he reached the kiosk he'd left a trail of people stunned by this force of nature, although a few may have just been concussed by his flask.

Presently a face appeared at the kiosk window. From somewhere under a shock of carefully tailored blond hair he beamed and looked at me with clear, Mediterranean blue eyes.

'Hullo. I'm Nigel St. Barnard' he announced, proffering a thermos, which we both stared at until he replaced it with his hand, which I dutifully shook. Before I could say anything, he continued... 'What a fine place ... do you know Crispin Rodgers from Twaddle on the Water? Fine chap, went to Harrow I think, not his fault of course. He inherited Hampshire when his uncle Percy died...he had a castle... 2 actually, now I come to think about it, but one of those was in France, hardly counts does it...have you by chance seen my thermos?

Ah, thank you...now I understand that there is a rather fine tea room here...Crispin had one in his, lovely muffins I recall...'

And off he went. I found him later regaling diners with accounts of his travels. He appeared to think the whole world was the size of Eton School playing fields and seemed genuinely shocked that they didn't know Margaret and Peter in Little Flange, even after he'd carefully described their cottage, two Labradors and daughter Emily who lives in Switzerland with Pierre and is expecting their first child in August.

Presumably every story he told started out with a point, but he went off at so many tangents they always seemed to finish with different protagonists, often in another country and occasionally involving an entirely different species. It was like setting off on a journey with a new set of directions given to you every two minutes by a caffeinated toddler. When he did finally finish a tale, it ended abruptly with something like '...In Tuscany, can you believe that?'

He'd stand back, arms slightly out to his sides and a look of such childlike glee on his face that you just had to acknowledge it encouragingly, with something like the verbal equivalent of sticking a child's scribbled picture on the fridge.

Later I saw him burst out of the shop in a flourish, juggling his thermos, wallet, ticket and a paper bag of whatever sparkly trinket had caught his eye and bound over the grass like an excited puppy, scattering children as he hurried to catch the ferry.

* * *

A nose appeared at the kiosk window, it was long, bent downwards and covered in grey hair. It was followed a moment later by the rest of its owner's face. A ruddy a man of advanced years but still sprightly and lean. After the usual pleasantries and ticket acquisition, he went away happy, but something about him was troubling me.

I served a few more people and took my break. It wasn't until I was halfway through my soup that it dawned on me what had bothered me about him. They were groomed. The hairs on his nose from bridge to tip, had been carefully combed and given a neat centre parting.

I appreciate that it is a burden to shave and might be painful to pluck, but grooming? Does somewhere sell little nose combs? Is there a range of tonics and gels I haven't heard of specifically designed for gentlemen with hirsute schnozzles?

I was unsure whether to admire his approach to personal maintenance or if it was just a bit weird.

* * *

She marched ahead of him, in a determinedly straight line that dared anyone to get in her way. The crunch of her shoes on the gravel sounded like an advancing army of the type that favours skulls and runes on its insignia. On reaching the kiosk she turned, sighed and stood erect and impatient while her companion huffed and puffed his way up to her.

He looked like the word obsequious sounds. Oily, soft and slightly damp.

I took him for the meekest man I'd ever met. He practically dripped with whatever the opposite of charisma is. I suspect she took his share and had a bit more in reserve too. He stood behind his, I'm going to call her wife because the only alternative would be jailer and she wasn't in uniform, wringing his hands while she demanded two concessionary tickets, one for her and one for Roger, MBE, in a voice that made wax trickle out of my ears.

Oh, how I loved that she just had to shoehorn in mention of his MBE. I imagine she warmed the cockles of whatever was left of her heart every morning in the reflected glow of his gong. I really wanted to know what he got it for, marrying her perhaps, but stopped myself because I could tell that she really, really wanted me to ask.

Later I saw them sitting close together in the tearoom. He was leaning across the table cutting her food up. She was looking away, admiring the view from the window? Embarrassed?

Was there a tear in the corner of her eye?

Then I saw the tremor as she tried to scoop her food up, the way she avoided eye contact and ate in staccato bursts. Always putting her fork down between bites so that her left hand could grab hold of her right, holding it still when willpower alone failed.

It was then I noticed the love.

The love he showed in his devotion to her. The love she showed him in the small nods of gratitude, the way she talked to him and to others about his MBE. Her pride and determination. His gentleness towards her and his small acts of kindness, like passing her a napkin without being asked when flakes of food dribbled out onto her chin.

Simple things done with sensitivity and grace.

At first, he appeared servile and timid to me, but I misjudged him. Here was a man coping, with fortitude and tenderness. She wasn't the harridan I had her tagged as either but a strong and independent woman who was fighting back against her own body.

I was quick to judge, and I shouldn't have been.

* * *

Then there was the time that a shelf collapsed in the middle of me serving a nun (really, I'm not making this up) showering me with books, I said a naughty word, and as the coup de grâce a vase of flowers spilt over everything. The last time my uniform trousers were that wet I was in primary school and Miss Statsford had just discovered a wasp in the toilets, so we were forbidden to use them.

I guess that swearing in front of nuns is generally frowned upon. I mean, there are worse sins, but I still felt bad uttering a wicked word in front of someone dressed as one of God's penguins.

* * *

To her enormous credit Alison not only serves everyone with quiet efficiently but through some magic that I have never understood she finds time to chat while serving them, putting them at ease and often getting to know their entire family history and what Neville and Eric got up to at Dora and Stan's wedding, the little scamps.

Remarkably, all this takes place in less time than I take to remember that the exciting shiny screen next to me is the till and wasn't there something that I was supposed to be doing with it?

I wouldn't want you to get the wrong impression about my time spent working with customers. I love meeting them, the variety of nationalities, the characters and the eccentrics. Like the old lady who holidays on Mull every year and goes for a swim in the sea, whatever the weather. During the warmest days of summer, when the tarmac melted, and birds fell like blazing comets from the sky I chanced a paddle in the sea and lost all feeling in my feet for a while it was so cold.

So good for her says I.

Good for the inspirational elderly German gentleman too, who was briefly separated from his family. Although clearly a little confused and forgetful he still had good English. He shook my hand and thanked me for my excellent museum (it's not mine), asked me if I was married (I am) and then told me he had three wives. As his daughter collected him, he turned back, winked and said... 'trouble is, I keep forgetting where I put them...'

Now that I think about it, maybe sinister is a better term than inspirational.

The world needs characters, eccentrics and people who care. People whose marriage is tested by illness and decline but for whom the love lives on. People who bounce, flounce and stutter around in a perpetual haze but in doing so spread boundless joy and raise one's spirits.

We could probably do without people swearing in front of nuns though.

* * *

One day the rain was heavy, the visitors few and my notebook was to hand. I'd been reading a spoof children's book, of the sort not unrelated to those with bright red beetles with black spots on them, which gave me an idea... Please note that for legal reasons these are generic experiences and not necessarily associated with any visitor attractions on Mull of our recent acquaintance.

Here is Peter. Peter is your first customer. He would like to buy a single ticket.
Peter has 7 Euros, 76 pence in loose change, a Polo mint wrapped in tissue and a £50 note in his wallet.
Peter buys a ticket and now has 7 Euros, £44.26 and a Polo mint wrapped in tissue in his wallet.

Here is Peter again. Peter now wants to swap his ticket for a concession as he has just remembered that he is 67 years old.
Peter now has 7 Euros, £44.96 and a Polo mint wrapped in tissue, and a large bruise.

Here is Jane.
Jane was behind Peter in the queue.
For a very long time.
Jane is cross. Jane buys a ticket with a £20 note.
Jane now has lots of little coins in her purse.
Hear Jane jingle like an angry fairy as she stomps up the steps.

Here are Bob and Marjorie.
Bob and Marjorie are on holiday with their son Tom.
Tom is 22 and works in Asda. Tom has a beard you could hide an otter in.
Bob asks for two adult tickets and one child's ticket. Bob chuckles at his little joke.

Bob is the only one laughing.

Here are Joan and Barry.
Joan and Barry are members of National Trust, English Heritage, Historic Scotland, The Caravan Club and UKIP.
Barry says a very naughty word when you tell him that none of these will grant them free entry.
Poor Joan and Barry

Here comes Doris.
Doris is 81 years old.
You know this because she has told you three times.
Doris is eating a Polo mint she found wrapped in tissue.
Doris is 81 years old.

Here is Hans.
You offer Hans a German translation.
Hans is from Switzerland, not Germany.
He has just informed you of this in a most efficient manner. See his moustache bristle.
Someone won't be getting a cuckoo clock for Christmas.

Here is Gary and his wife, 'the wife'.
Gary is wondering why you asked him if he required a leaflet in a different language. Gary is from Newcastle.
Gary and 'the wife' spend 12 ½ minutes inside then ask for directions to the tearoom.

Here is Doris again.
She is still 81.

Cliff and Tammy are here.
Cliff and Tammy are from America.
America is a country far away.
Cliff and Tammy love 'Scotchland'. They show this by wearing tartan hats that no Scotsman would ever wear.
Tammy thinks that Outlander is a documentary.
Cliff is drooling over the guns on display. See his trousers bulge.
Cliff and Tammy are very happy.

The Frasier family have brought Spot the dog on holiday with them.
Lucky Spot.
Spot was sick in the car.
Daddy is very cross. See his red face.
Mummy is washing sick out of Daisy's hair.
Clever mummy.

Here is Eric.
Eric tells you he has taken a picture of a white-tailed eagle.
Eric is very pleased with himself as he shows you a picture of a crow.

Today it is raining.
Toms face appears at the ticket booth window.
Tom says "Och aye the noo...It's a bonny day, nice weather for the wee ducks eh?"
Tom is from Romford.
Tom has stepped in something sticky.
Oops, naughty Spot.

Michael and Jenny get off a big coach with 41 of their friends.
They are all from Australia.

Except Michael and Jenny who are from New Zealand. They are very clear about this.

They are all on holiday together. Lucky people.

They have been to 14 castles, 23 tea shops, 17 museums, 6 distilleries and Iona. Michael and Jenny couldn't give a XXXX about yet another pile of bloody stones.

Michael and Jenny's bus driver is called Donald.

Donald thinks he is Jackie Stewart. See the sheep bounce.

Look out for the deer Donald!

Jenny has never seen the insides of a deer before.

See Jenny turn green.

Listen, here come Nigel and Susan.

Nigel is driving an Audi. See him park.

How lucky that no one else wanted to use those disabled parking bays.

Can you tell the time? The time here is 5pm. Everyone is getting ready to go home for supper. Nigel and Susan didn't see the sign saying you close at 5pm.

Nigel and Susan didn't see the rope they climbed over, and they also missed the CLOSED sign, closed doors and empty ticket hut.

Silly Nigel and Susan.

Nigel and Susan want to know where the nearest Waitrose is and where they can get a decent organic eggs benedict before the 8.30am ferry.

Silly Nigel and Susan have forgotten that they aren't in Brighton anymore.

Sylvie and Jean-Pierre are from France.

Sylvie and Jean-Pierre are camping. They are carrying all their possessions on their backs.

Jean-Pierre packed 5 socks and a spare pair of underpants for their 2-week holiday. Lucky Sylvie.

The ferry leaves in 5 minutes.

Have you tried running 3 miles with all your possessions on your back?

Sylvie and Jean-Pierre have.

Run Sylvie and Jean-Pierre, run!

TWENTY-FIVE

Fool's Gold

We needed to get away. Take a break from work, rain, worry, crowds, rain, the dawn chorus, rain and rain.

So, we booked a weekend off, closed early so that we could catch the last ferry, chucked the tent in the car and, in torrential rain, headed over the Sound of Mull and up to the village of Strontian on the shores of Loch Sunart, on the mainland of Scotland. An area as remote as any on Mull.

It was raining.

Heavily.

So heavily that we booked ourselves into the local hotel, a charmingly modest 1970's style establishment that suited as perfectly because it was clean, relatively cheap, friendly and, I can't stress this enough, dry.

The following morning the rain had stopped, and the sun was threatening to show itself, so we took a short drive up to the nearby Ariundle National Nature Reserve where we had morning coffee in a café that transformed into a restaurant in the evenings.

The welcome was warm, the coffee good and much advice was given about local walks. We had heard good things about the food so we thought we would return that evening.

First, we took ourselves off for a hike around the nature reserve, and very fine it was too. I even got to ford a river and feel like a real explorer. Alison decided that the bridge 100 yards up the trail would make for a drier, warmer and less hazardous crossing. Although I avoided calamity, I can finally admit that she took the best route. Not that I didn't appreciate tip-toeing through fast flowing, ice cold water, treading on hidden slime and sharp stones, and then climbing out with feet covered in sand and having to walk two miles back to the car wearing socks that felt like damp sandpaper. It's just that I didn't confess it to her at the time.

Since the world, or at least the little bit that we were in, had dried out by the time we got (hobbled in my case) back we went to the campsite and booked in.

Alison took our bags out of the car and I unfurled the tent.

'Alison' I called out. 'Could you pass me the tent poles?'

'They're rolled up in the tent.'

'Err...I think they must still be in the car'

'Nope, not here, they must be rolled up in the tent'

'Erm....'

We looked everywhere. Even in places where a bag of tent poles couldn't possibly fit. Well, we didn't look in our storage unit back in Stoke obviously.

Which is a shame since that's where they were.

Alison negotiated a camping pod on site, which turned out to be quite splendid in a rudimentary way, halfway between a tent and a caravan. We made a cup of tea, admired the view and generally pottered about until it was time to head out.

It wasn't raining, the air was crisp but not cold, we had a comfortable bed and a reservation at the restaurant we'd seen that morning.

What could go wrong?

* * *

The large windows of the restaurant looked down on the glen we had tramped through earlier in the day, shaded now by the steep wooded hills. Inside the beams were strung with fairy lights and candles in bottles flickered on the tables. We were greeted warmly and seated by a window.

We had arrived just ahead of the rush, with just one other couple were already supping wine and enjoying the ambiance. After we took our seats three other couples then a party of four filed in. Then a lone German and another foursome. We were all shown to our respective tables and...nothing happened.

It slowly dawned on us that the entire staff consisted of one harassed waitress and an elderly chef, plus one miscellaneous chap, possibly the chef's partner, maybe a passing axe murderer, who occasionally dragged his weary frame away from behind his newspaper to wander through the dining room to the lavatory. After a healthy wait we ordered drinks and were happy to chat about our day while others were seated at their tables and drink orders were taken.

It was when the menu arrived that we started to have doubts. It was handwritten in biro, in handwriting that was so hard to decipher that later we saw people eating dishes that we had no idea were on it.

We both ordered the pan-fried salmon on the grounds that it was legible. The waitress handed the menu on to the next table and trotted off with our order.

Contented with wrestling the menu into submission we sat back and passed the time watching a spider repeatedly abseil down one of the windows then climb back up. Then I read some poems by Charles Murray from a compendium I found among the various flyers and books available, after which I took a nap. Alison contented herself with playing on her phone, crocheting a fetching sweater and admiring the view. Just as our fellow diners were growing restless and demanding their drinks and menus our salmon arrived.

For a moment we thought our wait was worth it. The sauce was lemony, the vegetables were just the right side of al-dente and the boiled potatoes soft and buttery. The star of the show was the salmon, which was nicely seared on the outside but turned out to be raw in the middle. Being British we apologised to the waitress, who took it away...and so our wait went on.

By now our fellow diners had been seated for around 45 minutes and only one couple had been served. I selected another tome from the restaurant's bookshelves; the fact that they had such a selection suggested that maybe we should have recognised this as a warning sign.

Eventually our salmon returned with fresh vegetables and an extra dollop of sauce...which turned out not to be the lemony hollandaise but a mustardy version that was meant for the pork dish. I don't like mustard, and if I did, I don't think I'd choose to have it with fish. Alison does like mustard and confirmed that she wouldn't choose to have it with fish. We scraped it off and dived in.

It was cooked this time and aside from an occasional mustardy tang, palatable. Not fine dining, and considering the price it should have been better, but the ongoing theatre of fellow diners grappling with the strange Scottish custom of spending two hours waiting for an illegible menu and then wondering if their order would ever arrive helped fill the gap between price and value.

* * *

Sometimes we make decisions that we simply cannot explain afterwards. For example, we have no way of explaining why we chose to have a dessert. Maybe some primal need for calories decided for us, perhaps the raw salmon had stimulated cerebral neurones into misfiring, or, and I postulate this theory as an alternative, we were just stupid.

By the time dessert arrived a French couple on the next table still hadn't seen a menu and Tottenham were well into the second half of their 3-0 defeat of Manchester United, a fact I mention because it gave me an accurate measurement of time elapsed. We arrived at 7.30, kick off was at 8 and Lucas Moura had just scored Tottenham's second goal, so that's a grand total of 97 minutes waiting for a menu.

Why, I hear you ask, didn't they leave? The answer is that there really wasn't anywhere else to go at that time of night in a small town in rural Scotland, although I'm not sure that would have stopped me leaving after over 90 minutes without sight of a menu.

The desert arrived and was...interesting.

Apple crumble and ice cream is a wonderful creation. It can be a comfort staple bubbling over the sides of a Pyrex dish, a high-end fiddly concoction served with the ice cream perfectly quenelled, or shop bought and warmed in a microwave. We had good reason to think we were safe ordering it as the parameters were wide and the chances were high that it would fall somewhere in the middle of the acceptable apple crumble spectrum.

What we got was cold stewed apples with muesli sprinkled on top, served in bowls so hot we couldn't touch them. Admittedly it takes a special kind of genius to serve ice cream in red hot crockery without it melting but apart from admiration for the science involved it was basically the breakfast your granny would be served in her old folks' home, with ice cream.

When we left the French couple had just been given a menu, Tottenham had wrapped up a 3-0 win, were showered and on the coach home and we decided that it had been a more memorable meal out than a competent, properly cooked dinner in any number of alternative restaurants up and down the country.

Maybe that was its brilliance, an unforgettable dining experience; but not necessarily one to recommend.

* * *

After a night of mustardy burps, we surfaced in good time to pop into a different café for good, honest, old fashioned Scottish breakfast calories. The cooked breakfasts up here are high in carbohydrates, with potatoes cut, grated or squashed into different shapes then deep fried and served with bread, toast, fried bread or sometimes all three. All this alongside the usual eggs, sausage, bacon, black pudding combinations. Sometimes the more progressive establishments add half a grilled tomato or a couple of mushrooms to sex things up a bit.

If you don't eat meat they look at you with pity in their eyes and offer you extra potatoes to make up for the absence of square sausage and brittle bacon.

After breakfast we drove the north shoreline of Loch Sunart. It was stunning; remote, mountainous and sparkling in the sunshine. We took a detour to Ardnamurchan lighthouse, which sits at the most westerly point of the UK and is as remote and bleak, although beautiful, as that suggests, and then we caught the tiny Kilchoan ferry back to Mull.

I love the ferries here. I think this recent announcement on the timetable from the Kilchoan-Tobermory ferry sums up why.

'An additional return sailing will take place tomorrow on the above route. This is to help with a request to transport elderly passengers to a local funeral.'

Where else would a national ferry company do this?

* * *

It had been a wonderful excursion. Peaceful, fascinating and conducted at a leisurely pace. The calamities and oddball restaurateurs didn't faze us. We reminisced about Robert and thought happy thoughts about him. We held hands as we walked, laughed at our own private jokes and stopped the car every few miles to share a beautiful view.

It reminded us why we were here. It felt like nothing could burst our little bubble.

TWENTY-SIX

Just in Time to Say Goodbye

I used to be afraid of death. As a child I'd have moments of inarticulate panic when I'd swear my heart had stopped, despite all the evidence to the contrary. My mother would offer me the type of comfort that she was good at, generally a variation on the theme of 'oh for goodness sake Raymond, pull yourself together, you're not dying...go and tidy your bedroom.'

This didn't prepare me for the moment 80 or so years later when I sat beside her death bed and told her that it was okay to go, after we'd told each other, possibly for the first time in our lives, that we loved each other. We weren't close, not in the conventional sense. I suppose we did always love each other but feelings, affection and human contact like hugs and kisses just didn't feature in our relationship. At least we had the opportunity to say it before she died.

We so nearly didn't.

Working on the Isle of Mull has its drawbacks and one of those is being over 500 miles away when you get a call to say your mother has been admitted to hospital in Norfolk and isn't expected to last long. Aside from its remoteness, another feature of Mull is its propensity for its own weather system. While most of England melted under tropical skies, we had the remnants of Storm Hector to contend with, which meant winds that could pick you up like an errant crisp packet and deposit you in the next village and cause the cancellation of the ferry over to the mainland.

After some debate and confused calls and the storm abating, we managed to get an evening sailing and pulled into a budget hotel just outside Glasgow later that night. Once settled in we spoke to my children, the hospital, Alison's parents, my children again, and then we took a call from the doctor who had admitted mum.

He gave us grave news, honest and straight talking but compassionate; he wasn't sure that we'd make it in time even if we left right away.

Already exhausted and emotional we had to choose whether to set off and drive through the night or to get some rest. We knew the answer was rest; to go on then would be foolhardy and risk our lives, and probably those of other motorists too. But not to do so might mean missing the opportunity to say goodbye.

We compromised by setting the alarm for 3am so that we could get on the road after a rest. Alison talked to the ward staff and they promised to let mum know that we were on our way. Meanwhile for some peculiar reason I had an episode of Top Gear stuck in my head, one with Jeremy Clarkson wittering on about an expensive car and how he had used it to drive through the night from Cornwall to Yorkshire to get to his father on his deathbed.

Oh great! I had an oaf in a sports jacket making me feel guilty. Somehow though, just as I was thinking that sleep would be impossible, I was woken by the alarm.

We headed out into the strange twilight of an early morning in Scotland where the sun barely has time to set.

On we drove, exchanging pleasantries, admiring the early morning sun piercing the clouds over the Pennines, stopping for coffee and constantly checking phones to make sure we weren't missing any calls from the hospital. We made good time, even across the drudgery of Lincolnshire's endless flat and featureless landscape, down through Kings Lynn and then with a heavy and anxious heart we were suddenly in Great Yarmouth and pulling into the hospital. As Alison applied the handbrake I leapt up and out of the seat, afraid that if didn't move immediately I'd never get out of the car.

Fear, a companion since the phone call the day before deepened. The realisation hit me that I might be saying a final farewell to the person who, against all medical advice, brought me into the world; stubborn, single minded and frankly reckless with her own health, she gave me life. Maybe she wasn't the touchy feely type but she was responsible for my existence.

My words cannot do justice to finding that strong and independent woman laid helpless in a hospital bed; paper thin ivory skin and shallow breaths from dry sunken lips, a shadow of her former self surrounded by hustle and bustle, by busy people and bored patients. I held her hand, talked to her, saw her pain and felt powerless and impotent. In those minutes that became hours my mind wandered, to happy Christmases, to family holidays and silly games; to the person who was always busy and never accepted no as an answer, and to the woman holding her young grandchildren with tender love and huge pride. Thankfully they too made it in time to see her and say goodbye, fine young men now with red and tear stained eyes.

We sat, talked, slept, talked and ate, took breaks, went for walks and talked to mum; a strange twilight existence that contained memories and stilted conversations behind plastic screens. I found I would often zone out and let the hubbub of a busy hospital wash over me.

* * *

It was in these moments of reflection that I saw for myself what a horrendous mess we've allowed our NHS to become. Years of political incompetence, under investment, deliberate sabotage and our love of low taxes have left it in an ever-decreasing spiral of decline.

In a bay of six older ladies one was often crying or calling out for help, one lay with sad eyes watching us and when we took a break my mother lay dying in full sight of her. On the bright side we got to hear all about Eva in the next bed when she had visitors, and how her son left the toilet window open when he called in to pick up the pressure washer from them. Her visitor had the type of voice that could etch glass and was clearly under the quaint illusion that a plastic curtain suspended 10 inches from the ceiling was soundproof.

We were also treated to the oral delights of nurses talking to deaf old ladies about 'cleaning you up because you need to be changed.' There was no sense of dignity, no thought for the sensibilities of those they were sharing these conversations with because, well because flitting about in a rush was all that they had time to do.

If we weren't present, there was no one on the ward who could spare the time to sit with a dying woman or spend a moment consoling a patient whose dignity was left at the front entrance when she was admitted.

It's probably unnecessary to point out that the ward team were not at fault, although one or two need to remember that whatever grievances they have about not taking their breaks really don't need to be shared with the patients. Nurses and all the others who make up a ward team are not angels. Angels are heavenly beings who presumably don't require paying or rest breaks, and one assumes are enough in number to ensure that they can do whatever job it is that angels do properly. Nurses are human cogs in a machine that's being patched up with sticky tape and good intentions, forced to put up with crap conditions and harden themselves to the daily indignities that the lack of money or any credible plan of recovery forces them to accept.

In a moment of weakness, I picked up a copy of the hospital trust's newsletter and it was full of inane corporate claptrap that said nothing of any substance. For example: '**Strategic Ambition 7**: Make the best use of our estate and infrastructure.' Which rather begs the question (to a cynical old bastard like me anyway) in what sort of business would you ever consider not making the most of your estate and infrastructure? No wonder the NHS is in crisis when the managers don't consider looking after their property as an ordinary part of the business.

Just to add insult to injury, in 2017 the hospital's Team of the Year was – wait for it - the Car Parking Team. In a hospital of around 500 inpatient beds and goodness knows how many outpatient services, catering to a population of over 230,000 people and unpredictable numbers of holiday visitors, that employs over 3,000 staff in accident and emergency, critical, intensive and high dependency care, general surgery and medicine, maternity, paediatrics and neonatal services in a hyper-busy resource starved NHS, the team voted the best by 'a record 460 nominations from both patients and staff' were the ones responsible for ensuring that your Ford Escort fits neatly between two lines on the tarmac.

'When my Johnny was born eight weeks prematurely and I needed six pints of blood, and then our Derek only goes and ends up in A & E because he fell off the ladder and broke his leg, the silly sod, I was so pleased to finally come out and find Aunt Doris could park the Skoda outside for three hours while we all waited for Sharon to finish her appointment at the clinic.'

Said a completely fictitious person I just invented to make a point.

At least the team responsible for erecting the information signs didn't win. The ward my mum was on was mysteriously absent from them. Only on closer inspection, of the sort not entirely unrelated to waiting for one's wife to use the lavatory, I realised that they hadn't been updated since 2015, that's three years and counting. Oh, and when mum's care home telephoned the hospital, they were put through to the early pregnancy ward. I wish I was joking.

* * *

We often place an unnecessary burden on our NHS. Taking a break outside the ward was illuminating and saddening in equal measure. Heavily pregnant smokers wheeled out to quench their addiction, people using the A & E department to get their grazed knee treated, waddling children constantly drip fed confectionary and so on. I don't want to blame anyone, goodness knows people have enough to deal with in life without me judging them, but if just a few of us took more responsibility for our own health there might be a few quid left over to improve healthcare and provide better staffing on the wards.

Many NHS Trusts don't exactly help themselves either. Where mum was, they had a canteen for visitors and patients, run along traditional canteen lines; a choice of foods heavy on the brown end of the spectrum, relatively healthy options, a variety of snacks and grumpy staff. By contrast Addenbrooke's Hospital in Cambridge has a food court that last time I visited sported a branch of Burger King. I'm sure that selling concession space helps the hospital budget but condoning fast, greasy, fatty fried food really doesn't send the right message. The hypocrisy in promoting public health, healthy eating and reducing weight from an office permeated with the odour of deep-fried cow is frankly astounding.

* * *

After a long and restless nights bedside vigil we were treated to a mound of toast by the ward staff. I was pleased to discover that the NHS still runs on toast. In my days working for them, somewhere around 11:00am a stack of steaming toast, limp with butter, would be produced and with a cursory wipe of our hands down our uniforms (hygiene taking a distant 2nd place to free food for a student nurse) we'd all dive in. I learnt to love toast spread with Bovril and strawberry jam. These days I substitute Marmite for Bovril, preferring yeast to the juice of pressed bovine in my diet, although I suppose yeast could pass as a primitive life form, like protozoa or Jeremy Hunt.[xxiii]

I know Jeremy is an easy target but what galls me most about him and his buddies is the stealthy way that they are dismantling the NHS while claiming to support it. Any observer, whatever their political views, will know that the NHS cannot carry on as it is. The reasons are well researched, argued and known to almost everyone so I won't rehash them here, suffice to say living longer is costing us a lot of money.

There is waste in the NHS and yes, we could manage it better but ultimately it comes down to two choices:

1) Raise tax (and/or divert it from elsewhere but let's not get side-tracked by detail).

2) Dismantle it and opt for a private system along the lines of the USA.

Now, I subscribe to option 1, but I understand, albeit begrudgingly, that option 2 is a choice. My loathing of Jeremy Hunt and all the other baying suits on the right of the House of Commons is that they want to put mini malls and food courts into hospitals, commercialise everything possible, pull it to pieces and sell it off in bite sized, profit making chunks to the highest bidder. If only they'd have the courage to stand up and say so we'd all have an open and honest debate.

Which they won't because it would be massively unpopular, and they would lose the argument along with their comfy seats in parliament. Instead they sing the praises of the NHS, wear shiny badges proclaiming their support and pop into the nearest private hospital to have their shame surgically removed.

So, we have the shambles that health care is becoming today. What we witnessed wasn't unusual by any means, in fact my mum was probably lucky compared to some. At least we could be there, and the ward team weren't unkind, just overworked.

Ironically the one team who really stood out were volunteers. The hospital chaplain service really was amazing. They were kind and considerate, knew exactly what to say, gave comfort even to a grizzled old cynic like me, prayed with mum, offered respite and a calm space for private thought and reflection and didn't once shy away from being honest.

The hospital chapel is shared by all faiths and is a beacon of cooperation and mutual respect. There's no room for the luxury of theological debate when you are on the sharp end of human existence. In a building where fragile new lives struggle into the world every day and where loved ones exit suddenly, no one cares if you are Catholic or Protestant, Sunni or Shia. When you're comforting a mother who has lost her daughter it doesn't matter if you don't eat pork, eschew all animal flesh or think that all God's creatures are here for your tasty delight. What matters is the love, compassion and grace you show them, and if that isn't what religion is about then it means nothing.

Up and down the country volunteer chaplains, of all faiths and none (humanists usually) demonstrate exactly what is good and worthy in human beings and do so with scant recognition. No Team of the Year award for looking after your immortal soul when there are more worthy causes, like looking after your precious Audi.

* * *

The one thing the chaplains couldn't help mum with was the physical pain, but that was when the nursing team really came into their own. What I had no concept of until then was the dilemma that her pain presented. While she was sedated on medication, she was peaceful but semi-conscious at best. When the medication wore off or if she was moved by the nursing staff, she became more lucid, the pain jolting her back to the here and now.

How fucking awful is that choice, pain and the chance to say goodbye, a few comforting words, share a prayer with the chaplain or just to reminisce ... or no pain and no words of comfort or awareness of your surroundings?

Finding her in discomfort the nursing staff gently steered us towards pain relief and we willingly let them. By then mum was in a side room and fading. It was as if there was a celestial holding pattern, like planes circling an aerodrome until a slot became available. As she became less responsive and the inevitable end of her journey, at least down here on earth, was in sight, Alison and I spent the night taking turns by her side while the other kipped on a sofa in a side room. In the morning at around 10 am we shared a joke, something of no consequence, and mum passed away while there was laughter in the air.

We cried, placed her crucifix on her chest and sat with her. After a minute, an hour or a year, I gave her a final kiss and said goodbye.

* * *

In a world where we put money before care, political survival before compassion and cars before people death no longer holds any fear for me...it's dying that terrifies me.

TWENTY-SEVEN

Grumpus

The odd thing about being back on Mull and waking up to another day of work was the banality of it all. The same routine, the same suit, the same drive to work...but something deep down inside knew the world was now different and that it would never be the same again.

After 55 years I felt grown up. My parents were gone. My children had lost a grandparent. No experience in life can prepare you for such an event. Everyone's encounter is unique, the sum of the collective history of all the people involved squeezed into a bottle neck of intense emotions. For all the painful moments that lingered, happy memories were also released; the joyful times, the little signs of affection, the folklore of family tales grown pithy and refined in the constant re-telling. Memories surfaced for odd reasons; sight of my bright yellow pocket knife reminded me of the day I demanded smoked haddock from the fishmongers on my way home from primary school, attracted no doubt by the unnatural yellow colour. According to my mother's account I then refused to eat it, and such was her frustration that the plate was cracked over my head. She kept the plate with its tell-tale brown fracture, we found it among her effects.

Come to think of it I don't know why that's such a happy memory. I suppose because it became one of her standards, to be pulled out and retold with warmth and comic timing perfected over the years.

But for all the heartache and pain life went on, although for a while I felt that I wasn't exactly functioning on all cylinders. Alison was a rock, always there with the right words or instinctively knowing when to stay silent.

Life may never be quite the same, but it goes on.

* * *

We went back down South again for mum's funeral. After all the travel and tension, we arranged to stay at a nice hotel afterwards, beyond our usual budget. Time to relax and enjoy a bit of pampering. The room we were given turned out to be tired and the housekeeping poor. The final straw was finding someone's waxy hearing aid in a drawer.

In true British passive-aggressive style I told Reception how disappointed we were. Without any quibble or inspection, we were immediately given a room the size of Luxembourg, with more gadgets and shiny things than we had time to play with, like a coffee maker and a TV so big it wouldn't fit in our house. (Or my suitcase unfortunately).

I tried the remote control and the air conditioning sprung to life. I tried a different button, and nothing happened. Button number three, an exciting shade of red, succeeded in switching the TV on and the air conditioning off. I gave up and put it aside. The air conditioning turned itself on.

Meanwhile Alison was inspecting the wardrobe space at the other end of the room, I could just make her out from my snug little nest on the bed.

'I'm going to ... something something' she shouted.

'Pardon?'

'I'm going to...something something'

'Eh?

'I said I'm...Oh, never mind'

Cue an elaborate mime that I decided meant that she was either going to pretend to be a helicopter, skin a rabbit or take a shower.

With that she vanished into the bathroom, mumbling something about how I should have kept that hearing aid.

In two days we would be back on Mull, ready to pick up where we'd left off, but on that night we luxuriated in our suite, met an old friend for dinner and tried to figure out which of the 200 or so buttons on the remote control would turn off the TV.

* * *

Back at work we were tired and drained but pleased to be among friends and distractions. I took up my familiar position in the kiosk.

His face was tanned and craggy, with a limp and nicotine stained grey moustache drooping over a pair of cracked lips. On his head a corduroy Breton cap was doing a poor job of containing wispy grey hair that flapped around him in the breeze.

He was ahead of a party of four adults, at least three of whom would comfortably qualify for a senior concession rate. As they approached, I heard the tell-tale guttural rasp of Dutch guffawing.

My heart sank as he approached in the manner of a schoolboy being urged on to some minor misdemeanour by his chums. With a grim inevitability he asked for 'one family ticket please...see we are all a family...yes...?' and broke into a huge grin as he assembled the group with a sweeping gesture.

I gazed out upon three chuckling elderly faces and Mr Moustache vibrating with mirth at his comedy gold.

What is it about the Dutch that find this so funny?

At least once a fortnight a group will appear at the kiosk window and make the same joke. In advanced cases one or more will crouch down to make themselves appear child size, adding a dollop of physical slapstick to their jesting.

It's intended as fun but after the umpteenth time I confess that I can find it a strain to respond in a suitable fashion, but almost always I face it up with a cheery grin and smirk along while they trundle up the stairs congratulating each other on the originality of their material.

I'm not proud, but on this day, I was feeling a little jaded and just shrugged while ringing through four tickets.

That will teach me.

I discovered something worse than jocular Netherlanders, and that, dear reader, is jocular Netherlanders who think I've missed the joke and have the time to explain it.

I smiled while he went through the whole routine again helpfully breaking it down for me as if I were a dim eight-year-old who needed a friendly guide to navigate the world of adult comedy. As he reached the punchline he stood back and said.

'So, you see, I pretend that we are all one big family and request of you a family ticket, but really we are all grownups.'

As I opened my mouth, I remembered Alison getting me to rehearse appropriate responses when my sarcasm gene threatens to win in matters of customer service, so I paused, smiled and re-calibrated my reply into something appropriate. I thanked him and bade them a wonderful visit, although admittedly in the same tone that a hangman might say 'whoops-a-daisy' as he pulls the lever on the trap door.

I didn't mean to be a grumpy pants. It was just that the long season, deteriorating weather and stresses and strains of recent events had started to grind me down.

* * *

I think it's the introvert in me that has always struggled with coerced cheerfulness. Every family seems to have a painted aunt who appears on the doorstep sometime around Christmas with bright red lips ready puckered for enthusiastic kisses, tugs at your cheek and remarks on how much you've grown before leaving you to carry her cases, give up your bedroom for the week and join in with 'fun' games that your long suffering parents have long since tired of trying to rope you into.

Well, I did anyway and although she was a super lady in all other respects her insistence that games 'will be fun Raymond' was as predictable as it was inaccurate. I can forgive her because sometimes, despite my determined teenage gloom, I did raise a smile, but mostly because she was a pleasant old sausage who didn't once add the intimidating coda... 'Don't be boring...'

Oh, how I hate that.

From school friends enticing you to try alcohol and cigarettes to the forced merriness of the office party it's such an intolerable intrusion. I went through the cigarettes and alcohol phase because I was too weak to resist.

Later my life working in offices was roughly divided into two seasons; six months trying to find a credible excuse to avoid the office Christmas soiree and then six more listening to sordid tales of what Mandy did to Ken from Accounts in the car park and looking at instant photos of otherwise treasured colleagues in wigs and waving inflatable guitars about for no good reason.

Only on one occasion did I let my guard down and attend an office party.

It was awful.

I'd just finished digesting an over cooked slab of fake turkey when a haze of warm prosecco and clattering heels announced the arrival of a conga line. I was dragged from my chair to a chorus of 'don't be boring's' and 'it'll be fun's' and had to grip the clammy waist of someone I had no wish to touch, while my own midriff was assailed by an accountant who'd apparently come dressed as a sparkly Zeppelin.

After four minutes of this festive hell I was able to take advantage of a hilarious jape by the wag leading the line when he took it through a revolving door and amid the chaos I dived into the gents. Later I was coerced onto the dance floor because The Pointer Sisters were excited and singing about it in full voice. Apparently, I was boring not to sanction their excitement in the form of dance, so I shuffled around between colleagues who were sweating glitter and vodka. I eventually managed to get Y M C and A in the correct sequence just as the Village People were faded into The Macarena, at which point the people around me started a display of synchronised stomping and arm juggling worthy of a North Korean parade and I slid out of the door and drove home.

It's the same at parties. You turn up wearing your best Primark outfit, chat a bit, relax, silently judge the host by their choice of books and music and then someone proposes a game and you simply MUST join in.

'Oh, don't be boring...you'll enjoy it...'

Inside a little bit of me dies and I silently beseech them to reconsider my participation.

'Boring? Why am I boring in this scenario and if indeed that's what I am, then all things considered I'd rather be thought of as dull than spend every minute since I received your invitation dreading this moment, and then feeling uncomfortable and embarrassed for the next three hours while you chortle and snigger away...and besides which I've endured this so called "fun" for over half a century and it has usually been fun at my expense and not, and this is germane to my point, for me. So, despite your kind offer none of the evidence suggests that this will be the time that changes.'

What is wrong with 'Make yourself comfortable, there's some peanuts on the table, we're just waiting for Neville and June to arrive and then we'll play naked Twister. Feel free to join in but if you'd rather there are some books on the shelf, or you might like to take the opportunity to have a poo before the chilli works its way through uncle Albert'?

I found the best way with the office party was just to say no. No excuses, no explanations, just no, thank you I'm not going. After a while people give up asking. Well, apart from one boss who told me in no uncertain terms that it was good for company moral and team building and that therefore my participation in this voluntary event was mandatory.

That was the one year I went and on my drive home I decided that my job did not depend on me knowing the correct way to spell YMCA while jiggling about or on the amount of lager I could cram in before the free bar ran out.

The morning after the party he leered over me in a fug of cheap aftershave and stale beer and said. 'See, wasn't that fun?' with all the charm of a dead toad.

I handed in my notice shortly after.

* * *

It's memories like that which made me realise that for all the petty frustrations and antagonisms I may be experiencing, I wouldn't go back to the corporate world of meetings and mandatory merriment for anything...

...Anything other than a boat load of cash, my own coffee machine and a written contract stating that on absolutely no account will office parties, photo-booths, ice breakers, meetings that last longer than it takes to pronounce the word 'agenda' and team building days ever feature.

Signed in blood.

I decided that it was time to stretch my legs and count my blessings, which right then included a bag of hairy sherbet lemons I'd just discovered at the bottom of my bag.

I stepped out of the kiosk into the crisp fresh air. The wind that had whipped around for the last three days had died back to a gentle breeze that carried the sharp tang of winter. A buzzard circled over the bay and Alison appeared carrying two cups of steaming coffee.

Goodness I love that women.

I was about to tell her so when a jarring teenage voice caught my attention.

'Oh, my gawd it's like sooo old here, the place is literally like 100 years old or something and there's like... I dunno... all old stuff on the wall of like dead people and shit.'

Pause ...

'Ireland or somewhere... no no wait...the one with the like neat plaid stuff... Scotchland.'

I wasn't surprised to find her outside and on the phone five minutes after her parents had paid for her entry. She had the demeanour common to teenagers everywhere, listless neediness, demanding to be left alone and to receive constant attention at the same time.

I smiled to myself thinking back to my days as a teenager. A time when I believed that I was a grown up because bits of me sprouted hair and I was taller than my parents.

How wrong I was. It's a rite of passage we all go through, a confusing, scary and stressful time. I often sat on cold steps or wandered side streets while my parents visited whatever attraction caught their eye, usually the one that offered free entry if my Dad had his way. Eventually they'd find me sulking somewhere nearby and insist on telling me about all the exciting things I'd missed inside the Duke of Dullsville's stately maisonette.

Thing is, they were invariably more interesting than sitting on cold steps, wandering around the car park or throwing stones at trees which I'd been occupying my time doing.

Standing outside in the autumn sun I thought of Robert and his battles, of my mother and everything she had to contend with, including the teenage me, and although my rancour and bleak mood of late felt like nothing more than self-indulgence, it still troubled me.

TWENTY-EIGHT

Dancing with Devils

As time passed and our lives ebbed back into familiar routines odd memories surfaced at the most unexpected times. For a while they were mostly confined to disturbing dreams, the sort where you'd wake with vague memories and overwhelming emotions; fear, confusion, worry and anxiety. Then little things opened hidden doors that led in some inextricable way to my relationship with my mother.

Coupled with these thoughts was the lethargy, mental and physical exhaustion without obvious reason. The flare up of eczema, my irritation with inconsequential matters, the sleepless nights and dour days and the knowledge that it was all part of the process of grieving and of healing and that wishing it away doesn't help.

Knowing that I was unhappy.

I kept it to myself, but with characteristic grace and understanding Alison knew that I was becoming depressed and gently reassured without intruding.

* * *

'Depression is a common mental health problem that causes people to experience low mood, loss of interest or pleasure, feelings of guilt or low self-worth, disturbed sleep or appetite, low energy, and poor concentration.'

Depression really is amazing.

Imagine creating a weapon that causes different symptoms in every victim, that can span from 'a bit of a low patch' to being so severe that people would rather take their own life than carry on. A condition that can cause physical pain and mental anguish; that can drive one person to throw themselves under a train and others to slowly destroy their lives with alcohol or drugs, to seek the instant gratification of bad food and to repeatedly make poor decisions. A condition that some people don't even believe exists and others dedicate their lives to trying to cure. That makes a profit for pharmaceutical companies and dealers of illicit drugs, tobacco and alcohol companies, and for the charlatans that peddle potions and snake-oil to the vulnerable. A condition so varied that it often isn't diagnosed or when it is its often too late to be effective.

To make it worse it is a condition that many hide through embarrassment, fear, lack of understanding or pride. In some cultures, its existence is denied and unrecognised and in others monetarised and exploited.

Consider what would happen if the white coated bods whose job description is to create ever more inventive ways of killing or maiming people were to create a super-weapon that caused depression? If the same people who gave us the nuclear bomb and the land mine, napalm and polonium-210 tea bags were to develop something that could affect everyone, that was no respecter of race, colour, creed, religion, gender, sexuality or class.

We'd all be doomed.

And it isn't easy to remedy either. Attempts at intervention have included drilling a hole in the skull (sometimes your own skull), electric shock, exorcism, drugs in all shapes and sizes, isolation and counselling.

Effective cures have included drugs, counselling, gentle understanding, execution and throwing yourself off a bridge. If that sounds flippant it isn't intended to be (well, maybe a little). Depression is the predominant mental health problem worldwide, with over 300 million people estimated to be affected.

In 2013 it was the second leading cause of years lived with a disability worldwide, behind lower back pain. In 2014, 19.7% of people in the UK aged 16 and over showed symptoms of anxiety or depression, and in America 43% of executed prisoners had received a mental illness diagnosis at some point in their lives, depression being one of the most commonly diagnosed.

There is a clear link between social problems and depression too; particularly family stress, separation, divorce, social isolation, death of a loved one and unemployment. The very same factors are also known to increase the risk of suicide.

As someone who has been there, in a much more severe form than I experienced on Mull, I can look back on my own experiences with a mixture of embarrassment, fear and a sprinkling of humour.

We find ways to manage it and for a while as a single father I sought comfort in confectionary and bad, sugary and fatty food. An instant hit before the low. Not as destructive as some habits that people are drawn to, although my dentist may disagree. It was a coping mechanism, embarrassing and symptomatic of other issues going on in my life. As my waist band expanded, I withdrew into myself and resisted socialising, something that as an introvert I already found uncomfortable.

It is impossible to do justice to what depression is unless you have experienced it. If you have then your experiences will be different to mine, and to everyone else's, which makes it even harder to describe.

* * *

Like thinking through fog, you experience everything that's happening around you. The buzz of the traffic, the background chatter of a busy office, the shouts from the football terraces, the stories you read to the children, the bed you make and lie in, the pub gossip and the drone of the TV. They are all real, but you feel like you are experiencing them through someone else eyes and ears. You nod and smile in all the right places, process the spreadsheets, tick the boxes, bath the children, kiss your partner and chug on like a clockwork toy that just wants to rest but gets wound up every morning regardless.

Fatigue takes hold but you've no reason to feel tired, so you keep going anyway. Physical symptoms of depression are often ignored because it's seen as a condition that affects the brain, but the brain also controls our physical wellbeing, so, for example changes in serotonin levels affect sleep patterns and sex drive.

But you carry on, stiff upper lip and all that.

The sensitive ask how you are and of course you are fine, a bit down maybe, a tad blue, not sleeping well at the moment (smile), bloody weather getting me down, (shrug and smile).

The insensitive tell you to pull yourself together (grit teeth, force grin).

Sometimes depression has an obvious cause, post-natal or after bereavement people understand, even those who fall into the 'pull yourself together' brigade. Other causes are too many and various to cover here, but in a nutshell, they could be genetic, organic or in response to a life event or stress or anxiety.

Whatever the reasons and our symptoms, depression is real.

I came out of the end of my low patch and most of the credit must go to Alison for her fortitude and love, to my children, friends, family and colleagues for being there and never once suggesting that I 'pull myself together.'

Credit must also go to Mull, if giving credit to an inanimate lump of soggy land can be permitted. Every day I stepped outside of Mavis and breathed in the fresh air, looked at the picture postcard views, walked the hills, drove to work, watched a buzzard soar or a deer twitch its ears or looked up at the Milky Way I felt better, but what I really needed was a date with some endearing seabirds.

* * *

The Isle of Staffa is one of a small group of islands approximately 6 miles west of Mull. It's known for a few things, notably its basalt columns and the 75-metre-long Fingal's Cave, made famous when Felix Mendelssohn visited in 1829 and subsequently composed Die Hebriden, (Hebrides Overture), opus 26, based on the weird acoustics of the cave, which sums up all that I know about it as a piece of music.

In fact, the cave had been popular with tourists for some time. Or more accurately tourists with the means to travel to the Hebrides, charter a boat then witter on about it in their journals. Sir Walter Scott, Keats, Wordsworth, Robert Louis Stevenson, Jules Verne and Queen Victoria and Prince Albert all popped in for a quick squint.

These days once the season kicks off, a succession of boats vomit brightly clad and ill prepared tourists onto the small concrete jetty, where they either wander up the steep slope onto the main island in search of puffins and views or scurry around the basalt columns while clutching gingerly to the safety rope to peek into the cave.

We were travelling with Alison's mother and cousin, who had failed to think of an excuse quickly enough when we invited friends and relatives to stay. They did at least have the good fortune to visit during a heat wave and so early one morning the four of us lined up on the pier at Ulva Ferry on the shores of Mull's tranquil Loch na Keal, all brightly clad and eager to be vomited onto the small concrete jetty. After the cursory safety announcements, we set off past the small island of Eros, which as the deadpan commentary of our skipper put it... 'is notable for absolutely nothing at all.'

We'd chosen a day when the sea was mirror smooth, a slight haze made the horizon a faint band of shimmering blue and white and above the last clouds of the morning were evaporating under the strengthening sun. Despite being busy, the cave being closed because part of the walkway had collapsed during the winter, and the time limit imposed by the boat being too tight to allow much exploration, Staffa was wonderful. Its most notable feature, apart from Fingal's Cave, is that it is largely composed of hexagonal basalt columns, of the same type as the Giants Causeway in Northern Ireland. It's a splendid sight, from the boat as you approach and then scrambling over them to peek into the cave. Each one is a regular size and shape, but with varying heights. It made me feel like a pixelated superhero in a 1990's computer game, probably involving plumbers or hedgehogs, as I bounded from one to another.

Fascinating as it was Staffa was just an appetiser for the main course – Puffin! Well, we wouldn't be eating them, but the nearby island of Lunga, one of the scattering of small rocky Treshnish Islands, is famous for its puffin colony. Now uninhabited, Lunga was once populated by hardy folk who were all but marooned and left to the whims of the Atlantic Ocean and relentless wind. The islands village was abandoned in 1857 but there is evidence of iron age settlements and certainly the islands would have been important for the Viking settlers from the 9th century onwards.

Nowadays Lunga is of scientific interest because of the preponderance of rare flora and fauna that call it home. But much more importantly, to us anyway, were the puffins who flock there to breed and allow the brightly clad tourists in unsuitable footwear to scramble over the rocky shores to stick a camera lens within a few centimetres of their sad little faces. Considering the seemingly unremitting tide of people who visit during the season the puffins, and their avian chums, razorbills, are most accommodating. They nest in burrows along the cliff edge and pop up every so often to have a waddle, pop out for a lunch of sand eels and have their picture taken.

After a while I took refuge from the sun and joined Alison's mother below the cliffs where we were treated to the spectacle of the birds returning to their burrows from feeding at sea. In flight they were odd, lumpen little beasts, wings beating at a furious speed to keep them airborne, sweeping over us in their dozens from every angle. I don't think I was the only one who was disappointed not to witness two or more colliding in mid-air.

After everyone aboard our little boat had their fill of feathery cuteness, we all clambered back on board and chugged away between the forbidding volcanic rocks of Cairn na Burgh Mòr and Cairn na Burgh Beag. Once the home of Vikings, Cairn na Burgh Mòr hosts a ruined castle and a chapel from the Middle Ages. Alas tours don't stop here so we watched some seals lazily roll into the water from the rocks and listened to the gentle rhythm of the sea lapping against the boat and the less gentle sound of Germans using the on-board lavatory.

TWENTY-NINE

Look Back Like Leaving

The season was nearly over. The sun only made an occasional appearance and the evenings were cold and dark. We'd climbed, squelched, driven and trampled all over the island and beyond, yet still felt that we had barely touched the surface. We'd seen spectacular sunsets, views that left us breathless, mountains reflected in mirror like lochs, waterfalls tumbling from cliffs and waves breaking against hidden rocks. We'd picnicked on deserted sandy beaches, under cloudless skies and at times it felt like we had seen more rainbows than people. We saw deer, mink, otters, hare, dolphins, golden and sea eagles, adders, a pole cat carrying its prey, buzzards ad infinitum, and wandered through herds of highland cows and flocks of sheep with new-born lambs. We'd heard the stags roar, eagles call, owls' twit-twoo and cuckoos – well, cuckoo.

We'd made new friends and started to really appreciate island life, ambling along at a pace that allowed us to enjoy the views along the way, stopping to chat to people we passed in the street and learning to make do and mend. To borrow a phrase, 'getting Downwardly Mobile opens your eyes to really living.'[xxiv]

But an island, however beautiful, is only the backdrop for its people. The inhabitants of Mull are a hardy bunch, locals and disparate characters from around the UK and further afield alike. I've read somewhere that about 1/3 of the resident population are from outside Scotland, and even among the Scots many were not born and bred on Mull. There's a sense that the settlers have been drawn to a place of sanctuary, of community and isolation in equal measure; outsiders by choice and design. People who see a way of life that appeals and have the courage and fortitude to pursue it.

I'm sure that is a gross generalisation, but whatever folks' motivations we found everyone, from friends old and new, to colleagues, neighbours and strangers, welcoming and accommodating.

Some of the regular visitors seem to claim Mull as their own and exercise a sense of proprietorship over it. They spend time and energy needlessly bemoaning changes and improvements to island life and would prefer it to be set in aspic, perfectly preserved for the next time they visit. But the islanders know that they need to balance ascetics with reality.

Of course, some memories can be long. Grudges may still be harboured because of whose side your great great great grandfather fought on at Culloden or because of the clan your neighbour's ancestor belonged to. The Independence Referendum of 2014 divided friends and families and was then compounded by Brexit, when the people of Scotland voted decisively to remain within the European Union. But whatever appears to separate people, scratch the surface and you'll find they have more in common than what divides them. Everyone pulls together when they need to.

* * *

Mull has a rich history. Tales of warfare, clearances and shipwrecks; pilgrims, clans and castles; elegant houses and lairds are in the souls of locals and seep into the bones of settlers and visitors alike. Anecdotes of bygone times are seldom far from lips at the bar or at the till of the shop. Usually when I'm in a rush but there you go, that's Mull. It is an unhurried world, where traffic is mostly restricted to single file and island time generally means 'sometime soon...ish...maybe... if the ferry's running...unless Morag calls in for a cuppa of course.'

People stop to give lifts to hitch hikers, they offer to collect provisions for friends and strangers alike and lend anything and everything in the knowledge that it'll be them needing help next time. Although it is only a hairs breadth from mainland Scotland it's still very much an island where services and provisions are limited at times, especially in the depths of winter when the ferries might not run for a few days at a time. Petrol, bottled gas and medications can run short, so you rely on friends and neighbours. And where else would one of the prizes in the primary school raffle be a tonne of gravel?

Plus, you can still tell the season by the vegetables you can buy, and for a couple of people used to living within a stones throw of a supermarket, where the seasons were as artificial as the glare of the neon sign outside, that's wonderful.

Walking around you see the signs of make do and mend. Gates propped up, old doors made into chicken coops, half-finished improvements and homemade fences. It's a living, breathing land, undoubtably picturesque but for all the amazing scenery it is still heart-warming to see new houses, busy shops, thriving clubs, fish farms, logging, local artisans and crowded pubs.

It may rely on the fickle trends of tourism but even on a scorching summer day you can find a deserted beach or walk in the hills without seeing another soul.

* * *

Our house in Leek might as well have been a million miles away. We were fond of it and liked the town and people, but how do you leave somewhere like Mull?

How does one drive away, even if only for the winter, and not pine for the hills, lochs and glens? Who wouldn't wish to see familiar mountains capped in snow, to hunker down behind thick stone walls with a log fire while the wind rattles the tiles and to watch the sun rise on a perfectly clear, still and crisp winter morning?

Who couldn't resist the opportunity to stay in a remote cosy cottage over the winter to mind the site, do a little light caretaking and admin and to continue their love affair with this bewitching, beautiful island?

Us, that's who.

EPILOGUE

February 2019

As I write this, we've just come in from watching the Northern Lights dance over the hills. It was -4°C outside as we huddled under a canopy of stars to gaze in wonder at our first encounter with this amazing phenomenon.

The fire is blazing, the cottage smells of peat, woodsmoke and faintly of the dram of whisky that's waiting for me.

I'm not sure that we could be more content, or more smug.

At the end of the season we had a week away in the sun, an adventure that could be a book in itself. Back in the UK we foisted ourselves on friends and family to show off our tans and generally remind them that maybe us living over 500 miles away isn't such a bad thing after all. Then we returned to Mull and to work.

I'm caretaking the site, generally pottering about and doing whatever needs doing while Alison looks after the e-commerce and prepares for next season.

But it's not what we are doing that is important, and in some ways, it isn't about where we are, although on that last point the scenery is better than, to pick an example at random, Stoke.

What is important is that we are doing what we love, all because in September 2015, on our honeymoon, we decided to take a chance.

I don't think that either of us realised quite what a risk we were taking, but we met fabulous people and it led us all around the country and eventually to Mull.

The term midlife crisis has been used when referring to our decision to downsize and live in a motorhome, and then to move it to Mull, give up lucrative careers and enjoy life at a more leisurely pace. I'm sure the thought has crossed more than a few minds, even if it's not said to our faces.

And we're fine with that. When the time comes for my nearest and dearest to scrape the vinyl chairs up to my hospital bed for a few awkward words before I go, I want them to know that my midlife crisis was spent building memories, exploring the byways of life, on mountain tops and seashores, discovering hidden lochs in misty valleys, meeting interesting people, learning, living, loving and laughing every day. If that defines a crisis, bring it on.

We are content here at the moment. There is plenty to do and a season ahead that we are looking forward to. But we also know that there are new and novel experiences waiting for us somewhere else. We don't know where, or when, but then that's the beauty of this lifestyle, our ties are few and experience has taught us that a little risk can bring great rewards.

Whatever we do, wherever we end up, Mull will be forever in our hearts.

THE DANCER

Tribute to Iris Olive Rose Canham
1929 – 2018

I thought that writing the tribute for my mother was hard until I came to read it at her funeral.

* * *

As we gather to celebrate Iris' life and achievements it occurs to me that it's not something she'd ever have allowed herself to do. She just got on with things and didn't want any fuss. So, forgive me mum, if just this once we turn the spotlight on you.

It is a great privilege to deliver this tribute and to realise just how much mum accomplished, not just for herself, and her achievements were many, but also how much she enabled others to reach their potential.

She was born and raised in Tottenham, but at 11 years old she was evacuated to Cambridge to escape The Blitz. After a few months though she moved back to London.

When she found out that Alison was from Cambridge she took great delight in learning that her wartime hosts were known to

Alison's father; she took even greater delight telling us how the room she'd been staying in in Cambridge suffered bomb damage a few days after she'd left for London. Then with her characteristic wry smile in place she said 'No one told the Germans I'd moved back to London...'

Back home in Tottenham she finished school and became a Secretary and PA. She was proficient at shorthand and used it all her life to the benefit of others, including in this very church, as the secretary to the PCC for many years.

She faced a setback when she was taken ill with TB. Hospitalised and gravely ill for a time she took it in her stride, made friends and seemingly took the decision to embrace life fully. She went to the Isle of Wight to convalesce, a place she re-visited with me and her grandchildren. I remember those holidays with great affection, sitting with her on the chalk hills, with the sunshine over her shoulder and nothing but bird song and the delighted cries of her grandchildren playing happily; or all of us playing cards in the caravan with the rain beating time on the steamed up windows and the scent of fish and chips hanging in the air.

The thread running through her life was, of course, dancing. Ballroom, contemporary, Latin, Scottish country dancing, jive, tap, I could go on...or rather I could if I'd ever paid attention in the way that she wished I would.

But dancing was her world, a respite from illness, from health problems and a chance to forge her own path. She met her husband, my father, Don, through dancing ... perhaps the perfect partner for her, in dancing but also through life, complimenting and supporting her gifts with his own.

Through dancing she seemed to me to find her soul. Her spirit was on the dancefloor, particularly teaching others. From tiny pre-school classes to older people, from solo lessons to black tie balls, from perfecting gold medal standard sequence performances to dancing for fun or worship she always brought her own uncompromising style.

She was a lifetime Gold member of the International Dance Teacher Association, a fact that only came to light after I stumbled upon her gold badge. When I asked her about it, she shrugged it off with typical modesty.

Many here today benefitted from her dancing classes. Two of whom told me they are still dancing today thanks to her and they described her as an inspirational dance teacher... although I hope you had more choice in the matter than my sister and I did. We both remember staring out of our bedroom windows counting the children coming up the path for her Saturday morning lesson ... because an odd number meant we'd be summoned downstairs to 'make up the numbers.'

And she led dance in this very church, introducing Liturgical dance and drama ... I know that there are some representatives here today from then. And yes, I was involved too – sister, you dodged a bullet with that one.

Mum was also an artist and would paint for pleasure. A few years ago I took her to visit old friends, but it turned out that she had the wrong address... We eventually found the correct house because they had one of her paintings hanging proudly in their porch.

Later she would combine her gifts and use them to benefit people who have a learning disability. Firstly, at the Gateway Club; pushing an old pram up past this church to the hall, loaded up with records and her trusty record player.

Under her guidance Saxmundham and District Gateway Club performed at least three times on the stage at The Royal Festival Hall in London, no mean achievement. Then she started work at the Adult Training Centre in Saxmundham, overseeing dance, drama, art and work for adults with a learning disability.

To mum it didn't matter how much talent or ability you had, how naturally gifted you were or if like me you were born with two left feet. She knew you could do better ... and by golly she would see to it that you did.

She brought her own unique style to everything she did, a technique that served her well ... except maybe when it came to the kitchen ... She was the first to make fun of her own cooking ... this is the woman who proudly displayed her certificate for 3rd place for a fruitcake in the Saxmundham & District Horticultural Society show – and then laugh and tell you that there were only two entrants.

Dad was by her side throughout, her companion, a willing partner for demonstrating new dances and always on hand to set up the record player, carry boxes and act as chauffer. And she was by his side when he passed away in 1986.

If anything, she picked up the pace after he died, taking part in sponsored walks, writing, painting and gardening as well as organising art holidays for people with disabilities and of course still teaching dance in her spare time.

She taught her grandchildren to dance and was always amused by M_____'s failure to master anything but The Birdie Song Dance ... while J_____ collected certificates and medals. She also introduced them to the piano, being an accomplished pianist herself, where to her relief M_____ excelled ... and J_____ learnt how to play the Birdie Song.

They also remember with affection her room in Church House stuffed full of costumes and props, a Pandora's Box of delights to young boys. She would sit in her garden with her cup of tea and watch them play, smiling and occasionally instructing them on the correct use of the wooden sword or telling them what plants and herbs were good for treating the inevitable cuts and bruises.

She loved her garden ... especially if someone else was responsible for the gardening, and after retirement she enjoyed sitting in it when she had the opportunity. But retirement wasn't really for mum; she took on more and more ... once confessing to me that she had to retire to fit everything else in.

Gradually though time caught up with her and she came to rely on good friends, although she'd be the last to admit it ... among them T____ and P_____ who made sure she was coping and through their support she was able to stay independent for as long as she did.

Of course, she also had the companionship of her dogs. Lord and Lady, Chloe and latterly Charlie; and she was fortunate that when she had to move to Highfields Nursing Home Charlie could stay with her. She'd often remark that the staff would greet Charlie first and that he really felt at home...and if Charlie felt at home then mum did too.

* * *

Everyone who knew Iris will know how independent she was.

But sometimes the price of independence is ... independence. Mum and I didn't always have the closest of relationships; I guess when you've battled against the odds from an early age, overcome severe illness and defied every doctor and medical expert like she did, then you are entitled to a little leeway and to your privacy.

But as mum got older, we'd sit in her room at Highfields talking about 'the old days'. Alison and I heard tales of her mother making dresses, of her brother, my sister and our dad... of her family. Tales of Aunt Dollops who had enormous hands but was very kind, of nanny Westney, uncle Henry and Penny, Beauty and Roma the dogs and about her father, a fire warden in Tottenham during the war who wore a colander on his head to protect him from falling masonry.

Sometimes in those moments a shadow would pass across her face and you sensed there was more that she was keeping to herself. She was always a private person... Her name of course comes from the flower and a flower needs rain as well as sunshine to bloom. If ever a flower bloomed to its full potential it was Iris.

* * *

She was always a fighter, a trait she showed right up to the end when she again defied the medical profession and waited for Alison and me to get back from Mull ... and for her grandsons to be able to say goodbye.

She always had strength and she instilled a sense of determination and striving to always do better into everything she did, and into every life she touched through her long and varied life...

A life spent helping others to succeed. She gave much and expected little in return.

Thank you Iris, mum, for everything.

From me...

From us...

ACKNOWLEDGMENTS

It's impossible to list all the people who have made an impact on us and in some way helped Still Following Rainbows to make it to print. At least, it's impossible without the very real likelihood that we'd overlook someone and only realise when the book was printed.

So, thank you to everyone who has been part of the adventure, for buying Downwardly Mobile and giving such positive feedback, for messages of support and love, for being there.

Unless specifically referred to by name the characters in this book are based on our encounters, but any similarity to people living, dead or undead is coincidence.

Any errors, omissions, typos or other mistakes are entirely mine. Consider me suitably contrite.

I couldn't have done any of this without Alison, James, Matt and Dom. Thank you.

Thank you to the people we worked alongside in Staffordshire, to the folk in Leek and of course to the citizens of Mull for being so welcoming.

Thank you to our colleagues at work in Mull and to the people of Lochdon for putting up with us.

Thank you to our families. We wouldn't be here without you and we couldn't have done it without you. We may be over 500 miles away, but you are always in our hearts.

A special thank you to Adrian Nation for supplying the foreword. When I first heard him play I was emptying bins at a festival and he was standing in front of a painted neon elf captivating an audience that ranged from toddlers to pensioners, all held rapt by his virtuoso guitar playing and songs from the heart. I stayed and watched his whole set and saw from the number of high-vis vests on display that so did most of the festival crew. It takes a special talent to hold the attention of seasoned festival workers. From that moment I knew I wanted to collaborate with him in some way, only my complete lack of any musical ability whatsoever prevented this from happening. We may never share the same stage but at least now we've got to share a page.

The title of this book was taken from a song called It was the Sweetest Thing, by O'Connell & Love, taken from their 2018 album Minesweeping. The track contains the line 'are you still following rainbows...' which given the great number of rainbows we've seen on Mull seemed like a fitting title for a book. We had the album on repeat during our second season on Mull.

Every chapter of this book is named after a favourite song of ours. Our lives have a soundtrack and as you have read this far please do yourself a favour and check out some of the tunes listed below – you won't be disappointed.

1 – First and Last – Phil Burdett
2 – Darkness on the Edge of Town – Bruce Springsteen
3 – Where the Streets Have No Name – U2
4 – Say Hello, Wave Goodbye – Soft Cell
5 – Where Silence Meets the Sea – O'Connell & Love
6 – London Calling – The Clash
7 – You Brought the Sunshine – Dan Whitehouse
8 – Last Boat Leaving – Elvis Costello
9 – Four Seasons in One Day – Crowded House
10 – Up on the Hill – Dean Owens
11 – Ride Out in The Country – Yola Carter
12 – My Ever-Changing Moods – The Style Council
13 – Tillidh Mi (I Will Return) – Runrig
14 – These Days Are Mine – I Am Kloot
15 – One Fine Day – Carole King
16 – Living on The Edge – Iain Thomson
17 – Sing to my Soul – Martyn Joseph
18 – Joy Street – Songdog
19 – Radio Song – Simone Felice
20 – Take us Back – Mavis Staples
21 – Complications – Robert Finley
22 – Heroes – David Bowie
23 – Didn't it Rain – Sister Rossetta Tharpe
24 – All of the people – Simi Stone
25 – Fools Gold – Stone Roses
26 – Just in Time to Say Goodbye – Stephen Fearing
27 – Grumpus – Lambchop
28 – Dancing With Devils – Robert Vincent
29 – Look Back Like Leaving – Roddy Woomble
Tribute – The Dancer – Adrian Nation

NOTES

[i] Hertfordshire, England.

[ii] See Downwardly Mobile for a full explanation.

[iii] Posh word for shed.

[iv] https://www.smithsonianmag.com/science-nature/a-salute-to-the-wheel-31805121/

[v] https://www.streetcheck.co.uk/postcode/pa646ap

[vi] Research is perhaps too strong a word for the paltry amount of internet surfing and reading I've conducted.

[vii] Culloden, 1961, Pimlico - The Highland Clearances 1963, Penguin – Glencoe, 1966, Penguin

[viii] Not really.

[ix] https://www.hill-bagging.co.uk/

[x] Hamish's Mountain Walk, Sandstone Press, 2010 edition.

[xi] Some sources say Oran volunteered for the 'job'.

[xii] I've changed his name because he is a twat who doesn't deserve even the tiniest glimmer of recognition.

[xiii] Serial leader of right-wing political parties in the UK, and a bit of a tit.

[xiv] Handily summerised in Downwardly Mobile, available from Amazon

[xv] According to Google translate

[xvi] Sort of, it's a complicated story.

[xvii] Game of Thrones, I'm looking at you.

[xviii] Not really, I disposed of it in a suitable receptacle. Honest.

[xix] I haven't named the visiting team because that would be unfair to the well behaved supporters of Kettering Town FC.

[xx] The correct answer of course is Cliff Richard.

[xxi] And just in case you happen to be one of those intelligent, well-adjusted adults, the answer seems to be open to debate, probably New York but exactly where is the sort of question that occupies a few pages of earnest discussion online. Someone online suggested Avengers Tower and that was good enough for me.

[xxii] www.mencap.org.uk/sites/default/files/2016-07/Bullying%20wrecks%20lives.pdf

[xxiii] At the time of Mums passing he was the Health Secretary.

[xxiv] 'The Reason' by Andy Flannigan

Printed in Great Britain
by Amazon